Ideology and Libraries

Ideology and Libraries

California, Diplomacy, and Occupied Japan, 1945–1952

Michael K. Buckland
with Masaya Takayama

ROWMAN & LITTLEFIELD
Lanham • Boulder • New York • London

Published by Rowman & Littlefield
An imprint of The Rowman & Littlefield Publishing Group, Inc.
4501 Forbes Boulevard, Suite 200, Lanham, Maryland 20706
www.rowman.com

6 Tinworth Street, London SE11 5AL, United Kingdom

Copyright © 2021 by The Rowman & Littlefield Publishing Group, Inc.

All rights reserved. No part of this book may be reproduced in any form or by any electronic or mechanical means, including information storage and retrieval systems, without written permission from the publisher, except by a reviewer who may quote passages in a review.

British Library Cataloguing in Publication Information Available

Library of Congress Cataloging-in-Publication Data

Names: Buckland, Michael K., 1941–, author. | Takayama, Masaya, author.
Title: Ideology and libraries : California, diplomacy, and occupied Japan, 1945–1952 / Michael K. Buckland, Masaya Takayama.
Description: Lanham : The Rowman & Littlefield, [2021] | Includes bibliographical references and index. | Summary: "This book examines US-influenced initiatives to improve library services during the Allied Occupation of post-surrender Japan and looks at history of funding libraries abroad as a tool of cultural diplomacy, the development of free public libraries as a progressive political agenda in California, and an explanation of why in Japan library services were relatively backward despite exceptionally high literacy and very well-developed publishing industry and retail book trade"— Provided by publisher.
Identifiers: LCCN 2020035829 (print) | LCCN 2020035830 (ebook) | ISBN 9781538143148 (cloth) | ISBN 9781538143155 (ebook) ISBN 9781538171202 (pbk)
Subjects: LCSH: Comparative librarianship. | Libraries and state. | Libraries—Politcal aspects. | Libraries—Japan—History—20th century. | Japan—History—Allied occupation, 1945–1952. | Public services (Libraries)—California—History—20th century. | Public services (Libraries)—Japan—History—20th century.
Classification: LCC Z672.2 .B83 2021 (print) | LCC Z672.2 (ebook) | DDC 020.9—dc23
LC record available at https://lccn.loc.gov/2020035829
LC ebook record available at https://lccn.loc.gov/2020035830

Contents

Illustrations	ix
Figures	ix
Table	x
Preface	xi
Notes	xii
Acknowledgments	xiii
Photograph Credits	xiii
1 Introduction	1
2 Function and Form	3
Types of Library Service	4
Combinations	7
Resource Allocation to and within Libraries	8
The Librarian's Role	9
Notes	11
3 Cultural Contexts and Political Choices	13
Public Libraries in the United States	14
Comparison	16
Public Libraries in France	17
Notes	20
4 The California County Library System	23
James Gillis	24
Library Service	26
Harriet Eddy	27
The California County Library System	29
Training Librarians	31

Notes	33
5 Libraries in Cultural Diplomacy	35
George Creel and the Committee on Public Information	35
World War II	36
Office of War Information (OWI)	37
OWI Libraries and Information Centers	38
Notes	39
6 Libraries in Japan and the Allied Occupation	41
Libraries in Japan	41
Training of Librarians	44
The Occupation	44
Military Government	46
Japanese Librarians	47
Notes	48
7 CIE Information Centers	51
SCAP GHQ Civil Information and Education Section	52
Don Brown	53
Paul Burnette	55
CIE Information Centers	56
Okayama	57
Staffing	58
Notes	58
8 The Education Mission, 1946	61
Objectives	61
Leon Carnovsky	62
Philip Keeney	63
Library Recommendations	64
Notes	65
9 Keeney and His Plan	67
Keeney in California	67
A Unified Plan	68
Keeney as Library Officer	71
Willoughby and "Lefties"	73
Notes	75
10 The National Diet Library	77
The Imperial Library	77
Fahs's Proposal	78
Legislative Support for the National Diet	78
Verner Clapp and Charles Harvey Brown	79
Kanamori Tokujiro and Nakai Masakazu	83
Robert Downs	85

	Notes	86
11	The Library Law of 1950	89
	Nakata's Draft	90
	John Nelson	91
	The Library Law of 1950	92
	A Shadow	94
	Notes	95
12	Don Brown's Initiative	97
	Donald Nugent	97
	The American Library Association	98
	The Army's Commitment	100
	Downs's Survey	101
	Appointing a Director	101
	Notes	102
13	Gitler, Kiyooka, and Keio	105
	Robert Gitler	105
	Which University?	106
	Kiyooka Eiichi	108
	Sugimoto Etsuko	109
	Fukuzawa and Keio	110
	Strain at Keio	112
	Engaging with Japanese Librarians	114
	Notes	115
14	The Japan Library School	117
	Opening	117
	Faculty	120
	Curriculum and Resources	124
	Reference Workshops	125
	A Crisis and Dr. Fahs	127
	Rockefeller Rescue	128
	Notes	130
15	Afterwards	133
	California	133
	Information centers	134
	Philip Keeney	135
	Japan	136
	Other Americans	138
	Recognition	139
	Notes	139
16	Summary and Retrospective	141
	Historical Narratives	142

Libraries in Japan in Retrospect	143
American Librarianship	146
Libraries and Liberal Democracy	147
Notes	149
Appendix: Keeney's Plan	151
Transmittal Slip	151
Plan	152
Organization and Administration	152
Union Catalog	153
Suggested Procedure for Putting the Plan into Effect	154
Bibliography	157
Manuscript Sources	157
Publications	157
Index	167

Illustrations

FIGURES

2.1	Four types of library service	5
4.1	James Gillis	25
4.2	Harriet Eddy, 1902	28
7.1	Don Brown	54
7.2	CIE Library, Tokyo	57
9.1	Philip Keeney in Japan	72
9.2	Conference of librarians of imperial universities, 1946	74
10.1	Verner Clapp	80
10.2	Kanamori Tokujiro at the National Diet Library, 1948	84
10.3	National Diet Library leaders with Naomi Fukuda and Robert Downs, 1948	86
13.1	Robert Gitler	107
13.2	Kiyooka Eiichi and Sugimoto Etsuko	110
14.1	The Japan Library School announcement catalog, 1951	119
14.2	Robert Gitler and Phyllis Jean Taylor, later Jean Boucher, in the Japan Library School library	121
14.3	Japan Library School first-year faculty and students	123
14.4	Dr. Fahs at Keio University, 1953	129

Illustrations
TABLE

14.1   Japan Library School list of courses, 1951–1952   126

Preface

In December 1950, Robert Gitler traveled to Japan. His mission was to establish a permanent college-level school of librarianship. Forty years later, he told Linda Absher, a student interested in library services in Japan, that the story of the founding of the Japan Library School in 1951 had never been fully told. She initiated an oral history project, which I completed. Robert's recorded recollections were published as *Robert Gitler and the Japan Library School: An Autobiographical Narrative*.[1] It was his personal account, entirely from memory, and I had little opportunity or ability to corroborate his statements.

Robert Gitler succeeded in his mission, but it seemed an improbable success. I remained curious about the situation he had encountered and what other actors and factors influenced him. In particular, I wondered about Don Brown and a new law that mandated professional qualifications for librarians. Gitler seemed to have known little or at least had said little about either. After he died in 2004, I decided to try to find out more. Unexpected connections with California and the use of libraries in foreign countries as tools of foreign policy required additional exploration. Finally, examining these developments took me back to an earlier interest in *why* different libraries do and should develop differently.[2]

The principal outcome is a narrative of the roles of some Americans who were involved with libraries in Japan during the Allied occupation from 1945 to 1952 that was based heavily on English-language resources. A full account of Japanese library development during this period would be far beyond my competence. Two shorter narratives are about California and the diplomatic use of libraries. In addition, those narratives are framed within a discussion of the functional and cultural reasons why library services develop differently. Everything in this book deserves more detailed examination, but my hope is that the present account will be a helpful contribution.

As a librarian working in the United States, many of the people mentioned here were known to me by repute only. They were of an earlier generation. I came to know Robert Gitler well in his old age. Ray Swank was a colleague and a friend. Jean Boucher helped and encouraged me. Of the others mentioned in these pages, I met only three—Ben Bowman, Verner Clapp, and Robert Downs—only briefly and nearly fifty years ago.

I am very grateful to everyone listed here. I especially thank my friend of many years, Professor Masaya Takayama, for his assistance. A graduate and longtime faculty member of the school that Gitler founded and more recently president of the National Archives of Japan, he introduced me to Japan and to Japanese libraries.

NOTES

1. Robert L. Gitler, *Robert Gitler and the Japan Library School: An Autobiographical Narrative* (Lanham, MD: Scarecrow Press, 1999).

2. For example, Michael K. Buckland, *Library Services in Theory and Context*, 2nd ed. (New York: Pergamon, 1988); also, http://sunsite.berkeley.edu/Literature/Library/Services/. Japanese translation: *Toshokan, Joho sabisu no ronri* (Tokyo: Keiso Shobo, 1990).

Acknowledgments

I am grateful to many people, starting with Linda Absher and Robert Gitler. Robert's enthusiastic narratives about the past and Linda's proposal to record them led to his published autobiography and now this book. Jean Boucher, who as Phyllis Jean Taylor went with Gitler to start the library school's library, was very encouraging and shared materials that she had.

Many others provided assistance and encouragement. Colin B. Burke gave continued guidance on historical and security matters, W. Boyd Rayward and Melanie A. Kimball helped me use the American Library Association Archives, and Toshie Marra and Yasunori Saito helped with Japanese language materials. The wonderful collections and librarians of the University of California, Berkeley, especially the Northern Regional Library Facility and Bancroft Library, made this book possible. I am also indebted to the American Library Association Archives at the University of Illinois, Urbana–Champaign; the Rockefeller Archive Center in Sleepy Hollow, New York; and the Harriet Eddy Papers at the California State Library. Inessa Gelfenboym Lee and Anna Zaitsev helped with Russian texts, and Ronald Day, Vivien Petras, and Wayne de Fremery provided encouragement and helpful advice.

PHOTOGRAPH CREDITS

- Bancroft Library, University of California, Berkeley, Keeney Papers, BANC MSS 71/157, box 2:1: figures 9.1 and 9.2
- California State Library, Sacramento: figures 4.1 and 4.2
- Library of Congress: figure 10.1
- Rockefeller Archive Center, Sleepy Hollow, NY. Series 609 (Japan), box 145: 2737: figure 14.4

- Professor M. Takayama: figures 13.2, 14.2, and 14.3
- University of Illinois, Urbana–Champaign, RS 35/1/22, Box 33, Folder "Japan, National Diet Library Staff, 1948": figure 10.2
- Yokohama Kaiko Shiryokan (Yokohama Archives of History): figures 7.1, 7.2, and 10.3

Chapter One

Introduction

When Robert Gitler arrived in Japan in December 1950, his mission was to establish a permanent college-level school of librarianship at a reputable university. Universities in Japan were conservative, and this would be the first of its kind. He arrived knowing no Japanese and not much about Japan. He had only short-term funding and little time. Nevertheless, his mission was successful. The Japan Library School, of which he was the founding director, is now, seventy years later, the respected Department of Library and Information Science at prestigious Keio University in Tokyo.

Exploring the background to Gitler's task required examination not only of libraries in Japan but also some developments outside Japan, primarily in California, and the provision of libraries abroad as a tool of foreign policy. Inevitably, attention turns to *why* libraries differ, a more difficult and neglected topic. Eventually, although drawing primarily on English-language sources, enough seemed to be available to make a tale worth telling.

We start in chapter 2 with a discussion of functional differences in library services. Libraries serving different groups emphasize different aspects of service and so provide service differently. Conventionally, there are four types of library. A typical public library branch is recognizably different from a typical university library, which, in turn, differs from a specialized corporate library or a primary school library. Libraries have major differences in their collections, use of space, the manner in which services are provided, and in their roles in society.

Also, just as people living in groups tend to have cultural similarities, libraries tend to be more similar within the same cultural context. Libraries in any context tend to reflect cultural characteristics of their context (chapter 3).

Chapters 4 through 14 provide three historical narratives: first, an example of the development of library services within a single state, California (chapter 4); then, the provision of services by one country within another country to achieve a cultural influence (chapter 5); and then, a much longer account of efforts at developing libraries where two different governments with two different cultures were coexisting in the same country during the Allied occupation of Japan after World War II, from 1945 to 1952 (chapters 6–14). Some notes on what happened to the individuals and institutions in those narratives after 1952 follow (chapter 15). Finally, chapter 16 draws some conclusions.

We may note that, over time, practices in library services gradually have become more standardized nationally and internationally. They differ now less than they did in 1950 and differed then less than in 1900 or earlier. Also, during the period this book covers, roughly the first half of the twentieth century, library collections were on paper or other "local" media, such as microfilms and drawings, whereby both reader and document must be in the same place if anything is to be read. Local collections, therefore, were more important than now with digital documents, whereby a document may be stored in one place but read in a temporary display in another place.

The next chapter explores some relationships between differing forms of library service and the differing purposes for which they are designed.

Chapter Two

Function and Form

Each library is unique, of course, just as each person is different. Humans have varying physical and cultural characteristics and a tendency toward similarities within communities. Because humans are very complex and variations between them are often very small, meaningful comparative statements about different groups are difficult. Discourse in social sciences is made simpler and easier by using a few real or imaginary examples that are assumed to be usefully representative of some type worth discussing. We might refer to a "typical Frenchman," for example. When this is done, the example is called an archetype. Such archetypes are not usually particular persons selected as representative, but imaginary constructs based on selected characteristics and statistical data. It is meaningful to state, for example, that the households in some region have on average one and one-half children, even though there are no half children.

The use of archetypes also provides a convenient basis for examining how and why libraries differ. Traditionally, libraries have been divided into four types: academic libraries in college and university libraries; public libraries, mostly providing recreational and educational reading; school libraries in primary and secondary schools; and "special" libraries, meaning specialized libraries in corporate settings, especially in firms engaged in commerce, manufacturing, or research and development, but also in government agencies and other organizations. Special libraries also are known as documentation centers or information centers. These four types of library are recognizably different. One would not mistake one type for another, and librarians tend to specialize in one of these types of library throughout their careers.

TYPES OF LIBRARY SERVICE

In principle, the four traditional types of library offer the same types of service. What distinguishes them is their differing emphases on different services. Therefore, we can move our analysis from types of library to types of library service, and we use differing kinds of readers' needs for service to construct four archetypal styles of service using a distinction between topics of interest and sources of interest.[1]

We use *topic* to refer to whatever a library user wants to read about. The reader may want to see a statement of fact, an explanation, a discussion, or any other kind of narrative. *Source* includes any kind of document, book, data set, or any other form of record.

Both the topic and the source may be more or less *particular*, meaning more or less precisely specified. The topic might be defined very exactly. For example, what is the melting point of lead, or what was the population of Klagenfurt in 1900? It might, however, be more general, such as a guide to Impressionist painting or an introduction to retirement planning. And, at the other end of this scale, it simply might be a request for a topic genre, such a detective novel, a romance, or a travelogue. In an extreme case, the topic may not matter much or at all if the text is amusing, inspiring, or otherwise worth attention.

Likewise, how far the library user is interested in a particular source varies. It may be that any source is acceptable if it provides what the reader seeks. Sometimes a particular author or text is wanted. At the extreme, only one particular copy of a manuscript or a particular edition of a published work is needed, and no other source can be substituted for it. Individual copies of manuscripts ("witnesses") are important because errors, additions, and corrections are introduced when texts are transcribed, making each copy different. And a biographer, for example, will want to see any comments written in the margins of the individual books that the subject of the biography owned.

If we combine just two degrees of how particularly the topic is specified and two degrees of how particularly the source is specified, the simple two-by-two matrix shown in figure 2.1 results. The four combinations of the two variables describe four different styles of library service and are labeled as fact-checking, historical research, recreational reading, and current awareness.

Fact-checking, in the upper left box, involves particular topics for which any responsive source will serve. A small collection of up-to-date and trustworthy reference works covering the topics most often of interest is used. These works can be discarded as more reliable or more up-to-date alternatives are acquired. Exceptional queries not satisfied by the limited collection can be referred elsewhere. This library service style is characterized by quite

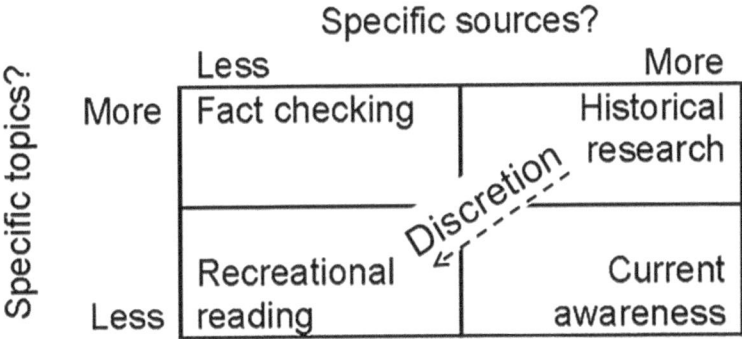

Figure 2.1. Four types of library service.

specific queries and dependence on a modest collection of relatively trustworthy documents. This style is seen in the reference section of any library.

Current awareness, in contrast, in the lower right box, tends to involve scanning particular specialized alerting services for news of any topic of interest, especially unforeseen developments. Commonly the source is a periodical such as a technical magazine, a bibliography of new publications, or a listing of new patents, legislative proposals, or regulations. The absence of new developments also can be significant, especially in a competitive situation.

These two types of service have been given different names over the years. In the information retrieval literature, they are known as ad hoc search and filtering, respectively. They are of additional interest here for two reasons. First, the characteristics of fact-checking (particular topics, any responsive source) and current awareness (particular sources, any relevant news) can be seen as symmetrical. Second, the combination of these two services is characteristic of special libraries, which illustrates well the distinction between type of library and type of service.

However, two other service combinations of topics and documents are of more importance for our discussion.

Historical research, or any other rigorous research requiring exhaustive attention to prior literature, creates severe demands on libraries. Readers tend to have very particular needs, and access to specific particular documents is of critical importance. Researchers need to see the exact text of particular documents to find out what that author wrote on that occasion in order to infer what the author meant at that time. Also, for any particular topic, examination of all texts, or as many as possible, relating to that particular topic may be needed to establish the intellectual history of that topic. This exhaustive library style is dominated by the need for an unlimited range of particular documents. Substitutions would be unacceptable or, at least, regarded with suspicion. Excellent bibliographic apparatus is needed to characterize each document and each topic as far as possible.

This is very burdensome for large libraries, as is reflected in the complexity of their classification schemes and the Library of Congress subject headings. No library can be too large, and only surplus duplicates would be discarded. Precise cataloging and bibliographical description are needed, but, because urgency usually is not great, less-expensive closed access book shelving is relatively tolerable. In reality, exhaustive completeness is neither affordable nor feasible, so collaborative infrastructure in the form of interlibrary loan agreements, coordination in collection development, "union" catalogs recording the holdings of multiple libraries' collections, and reliable bibliographical descriptions enumerating all known documents becomes important. Scholars have to accept that they will need to use multiple other libraries as an extension of their own library. The idea that any library can obtain any document is a powerful part of the library's image.

Just as a current awareness service can be seen as an inverse of a fact-checking service, the inverse of library service for historical research can be seen in provision for *recreational reading*. Public libraries, especially branch libraries, specialize in attractive examples of genres of literature (e.g., crime, romance, science fiction, and historical novels) and readable introductions to topics of general interest, such as history, hobbies, travel, and self-improvement. Books are freely discarded to save space when they cease to be popular. Because readers tend to be interested in books with certain characteristics rather than in particular works, similar works may be equally acceptable. There is latitude for them to be tolerable substitutes for each other. Most bookshops are in this style. In this situation the particular author, title, and edition are less relevant than whether the documents are attractive and compatible with the community served. Librarians are more likely to be asked for a type of book than for a particular book. Certain genres such as adventure, crime, romance, self-improvement, and Westerns remain popular. A salient feature is that the readers' choice is within a selection already shaped by the provider's social and educational agenda. Readers' access to the shelves is strongly preferred to facilitate relatively subjective choices. School libraries have similar characteristics when the education is didactic, meaning that the emphasis is on instruction rather than discovery.

The distinction between these last two styles has a special and central significance for the rest of this book. We can view them as being at the opposite ends of a spectrum. At the historical research library end of that spectrum, we find the largest university libraries and national libraries. The size and complexity of these institutions require the highest technical expertise as well as a heavy investment in buildings and collections. Because of their needs and resources, these large libraries tend to lead in the development of technical standards and the deployment of new technology. In effect, the severe technical challenges of developing and maintaining them dominate. Because the readers' needs are so particular, the librarians and library funders have limited discretion: at any given state of technical development and budget, they provide library service at the scale they can afford with the technical expertise that they have. In this sense, this style of library service has a relatively mechanical and technical tendency driven by the academic program of the institution.

At the other end of this spectrum, in contrast, where the choice of particular books is less specified and alternative texts more easily substituted, there is more discretion in book selection. To be sure, there will still be tension and accommodation between readers' demands for specific books and librarians' preferred selections, but recreational and didactic educational reading allow more flexibility in book selection, both in choice of topics and choice of books. In particular, the selection of books for children and young adults in a public library allows considerable latitude for the social and cultural values of the providers. These values may differ from those of the community served. Librarians have more discretion in book selection and in their recommendations for readers. Complaints about book selection are more likely to be about taste and propriety and to be more frequent in school libraries and public libraries than in other types of library. In other words, one can expect ideological considerations to be more salient in the provision of recreational and educational reading than in exhaustive research libraries.

COMBINATIONS

These four styles of library service show that form follows function. Caution is needed, however, because in practice all libraries combine all four styles of service. What differentiates types of library is the very different emphases. As already noted, private sector corporate libraries typically combine a fact-checking style service with a current awareness service, monitoring changes in the external environment. Mid-twentieth century public libraries in Britain would commonly provide service in three different styles: a collection for recreational and educational reading would be the primary service, but a newspaper and magazine reading room offered a kind of alerting service; and a reference collection, often with a reference librarian, supported fact-finding and fact-checking. Only the central library of the largest cities, such as Birmingham and Manchester, also would support historical research. The New York Public Library has its famous research collections organizationally separate from the numerous branch libraries offering reading for recreation and education. National libraries follow the historical research library style. So do university libraries, but often in tension with independent small departmental libraries more in the style of special libraries. They may, if enlightened, also provide some support for students' recreational reading.

RESOURCE ALLOCATION TO AND WITHIN LIBRARIES

A library's profile of services derives from the allocation of resources to and within the library. This is a matter of political and managerial sponsorship. The external environment—some social, political, or corporate situation—possesses resources, some of which can be allocated for the support of a library service, but other possible uses always are competing for these resources. Of importance, unlike a commercial service in which usage generates resources through customers' payments, libraries are a public service characterized by a separation of use from the allocation of resources. A university president, local government authority, or corporate management allocates resources to the library; library management deploys the resources according to its best judgment; and the population served chooses whether and how to use the library. This pattern, usual for government services, sometimes is referred to as "the library model." It does not follow that the three roles (funders, managers, and users) are independent. In practice each can and does influence the other two. Public library users, for example, are also voters, and voters determine who is elected to raise taxes and allocate local government resources. Also, services are designed for the users and for use, so users' preferences matter; and book selection caters, at least in part, to expected demand. But book selection also reflects what librarians think would be good for the readers. It is a paternalistic role. Each party has an interest in a successful library, but, of course, what constitutes success depends on ideas about what is the proper purpose of the library.[2]

A distinction can be made between the allocation of resources to a library by a funding authority and the deployment of resources within the library by the chief librarian, but one would expect discussion, negotiation, and agreement. The library director requests funding for specific purposes, and the funders give funding for a set of programs. However, library services are labor intensive, and several factors cause a diffusion of responsibility. Libraries' organization structures are hierarchical; larger libraries are commonly geographically decentralized for the convenience of users; and some degree of specialization and division of labor is normal. Further, because the effects of library service generally are not clear, the consequences of individual decisions also are not clear. This combination of factors means that responsibility for decision making becomes diffused, especially in book selection and the detailed deployment of staff time. Although individual decisions may be small in import, they have a cumulative effect and will reflect the personal ideas and values of many different individuals. This is a characteristic of labor-intensive human services.³

THE LIBRARIAN'S ROLE

It follows from the political nature of the library funding and the diffusion of decision making that librarians, especially library directors, have a mediating role in influencing the allocation of resources to and within the library. That role will depend on differing ideas about the purpose of the library. If the library is seen primarily as a collection to be conserved, then the librarian's role is custodial. It is a clerical or technical role with some bibliographical skills in identifying, describing, and conserving documents.

But if the library's role is seen as recreational or educational, then library staff will have views concerning what is proper, moral, and compatible with the standards of the community. Disagreements will concern which books are suitable and which are unacceptable. There may be protests. Librarians may choose to reduce disagreements by excluding what may be controversial. Librarians may decide that some material is so important that it should be included even if some readers find it offensive. One view is that librarians should be neutral, but it is more a matter of tolerance than neutrality.

If we look for an ideal, friendly, knowledgeable librarian who knows the collection and is familiar with its readers, we might start with the scholar librarian of seventeenth- and eighteenth-century Europe when collections were so much smaller than now. Libraries had a more museum-like existence with few readers. The occasional need of library visitors to select or locate a book was solved by the librarian with his intimate familiarity with the collection and knowledge of its subject matter.⁴

Problems arise, however, with even the best human librarian as a service provider. There are limits to how many topics can be understood, how large a collection can be known well, and how many readers can be helped in a day. In engineering terms, a human librarian does not scale well, and, as in other service situations, only self-service and mechanization scale affordably. Worse, human librarians are prone to catastrophic failure: the librarian may leave or die or become forgetful.

The origin of "library science," by that name, was a response to these problems. Around the end of the eighteenth century, many monasteries in Europe were closed and their libraries confiscated. In Bavaria, two hundred monastic libraries were sent to Munich to be added to the royal library, and the library staff were unable to cope with this flood of material. Martin Schrettinger (1772–1851), a monk turned librarian, solved the problem. Schrettinger understood that technical systems were needed to enable readers (as well as librarians) to find what they needed by themselves quickly and easily. It was for the technical guidelines that he developed that he coined the phrase *Bibliothek-Wissenschaft* (in English, "library science") in a textbook he published in 1808.

His book began with "A 'library' is a large collection of books *whose organization enables every knowledge seeker* to use every treatise it contains without unnecessary delay according to his needs."[5] The central idea was that with a unique identifier for each volume, a good catalog, and a link from the catalog record to the volume's shelf location, anyone could make satisfactory use of the collection whatever the arrangement of books on the shelves without requiring the help of a librarian. His particular solution was to provide shelf arrangement in broad subject clusters complemented by an author catalog, a shelf list, and, later, a subject catalog. In effect, the library catalog becomes a surrogate for the librarian, fixing the librarian's knowledge and culture into the technical machinery of the library. Schrettinger seems to have been the first to propose formal professional education programs in library science.[6]

The most respected German scholar librarian at that time, Friedrich Albert Ebert (1791–1834), angrily denounced Schrettinger for undervaluing the human librarian. However, Ebert fell off a ladder in his library and died, thereby demonstrating the risk of depending on scholar librarians and the advantage of a catalog embodying the librarians' bibliographical knowledge. Reliance on the technology of catalogs as a surrogate for the human librarian does not remove the librarian's personal cultural values. Rather, it fixes the librarian's knowledge and cultural values into the seemingly impersonal technical machinery of the library.

The techniques and technology of library service are quite generic. A competent librarian easily can adjust to the procedures of another library, a different type of library, or a library in another country. This chapter has been concerned with structural issues, with how different kinds of library service suit different types of need. This provides a functional explanation of library differences. But another very powerful force for differences in library service remains: the political choices concerning how much of each kind of service to provide. These choices reflect social agendas, so they can be expected to vary from one cultural context to another and also to change over time as cultural values and political priorities change. One does not need to be a Marxist to note that allocations of resources tend to reflect the agendas of those who have the power to make the allocation. The next chapter is concerned with the influences of social context and cultural values on library services.

NOTES

1. This section is based on Michael K. Buckland, "On Types of Search and the Allocation of Library Resources," *Journal of the American Society for Information Science* 30, no. 3 (May 1979): 143–47.

2. For a fuller discussion, see Michael K. Buckland, *Library Services in Theory and Context*, 2nd ed. (Oxford: Pergamon, 1988), chaps. 11 and 12; also, http://sunsite.berkeley.edu/Literature/Library/Services/. On how political and economic processes are related, see Albert O. Hirschman, *Exit, Voice, and Loyalty; Responses to Decline in Firms, Organizations, and States* (Cambridge, MA: Harvard University Press, 1970).

3. Yeheskel Hasenfeld, *Human Service Organizations* (Englewood Cliffs, NJ: Prentice-Hall, 1983).

4. See Jeffrey Garrett, "Redefining Order in the German Library, 1775–1825," *Eighteenth-Century Studies* 33, no. 1 (Fall 1999): 103–23, http://www.jstor.org/stable/30053317; Michael K. Buckland, "Library Technology in the Next Twenty Years," *Library Hi Tech* 35, no. 1 (2017): 5–10; also, http://escholarship.org/uc/item/9gs9p655; Michael K. Buckland, "The Relationship between Human Librarians and Library Systems: Catalogs and Collections," in *Estudios de la información: teoría, metodología y práctica*, cood. Georgina Araceli Torres Vargas (Mexico City: UNAM, Instituto de Investigaciones Bibliotecológicas y de la Información, 2018), 91–105, http://ru.iibi.unam.mx/jspui/handle/IIBI_UNAM/L158; and Uwe Jochum, *Bibliotheken und Bibliothekare 1800–1900* (Wurzburg: Konigshausen und Neumann, 1991).

5. Martin Schrettinger, *Versuch eines vollständigen Lehrbuches der Bibliothek-Wissenschaft* (Munich: author, 1808), 11, http://archive.org/details/bub_gb_x2qePg9yKNkC Schrettinger. Translation from Garrett, "Redefining Order," 116, emphasis added.

6. J. Periam Danton, "Corrigendum and Addendum to a Footnote on Library Education History," 73–78, in *Essays and Studies in Librarianship Presented to Curt David Wormann on His Seventy-Fifth Birthday*, edited by M. Nadav and J. Rothschild (Jerusalem: Magnes Press, Hebrew University, 1975).

Chapter Three

Cultural Contexts and Political Choices

Just as human communities have both cultural and genetic characteristics, so library services contain cultural as well as technical aspects. The cultural aspects are reflected in the choices made concerning the type and scale of services to provide. Libraries are service organizations ordinarily funded by a large organization, such as a local government, an educational institution, or a commercial corporation, to advance the purposes of the larger organization. Libraries, therefore, are funded through political rather than commercial mechanisms. The amount of funding and its deployment within the library follow the objectives, values, and priorities of the funding agency. The users of a library are not directly responsible for the library's income or the profile of service, but they may have substantial indirect influence. Public libraries' users are also voters who elect local government officials to implement particular policies. University libraries' users include professors who also serve on influential campus committees and occupy the top positions in academic administration.

As noted in the previous chapter, library provision for recreational and educational purposes in public and school libraries is influenced more by the providers' cultural values than in academic research libraries or corporate special libraries. Consequently, examination of public library services in different countries should provide additional insight into the effects of cultural context on how and why libraries differ. We could consider, for example, how ideas about the proper role of public library service in the United States might differ from ideas about library services in, say, France or Japan.

Chapter 3
PUBLIC LIBRARIES IN THE UNITED STATES

A rich literature is available on the ideas that drove the development of public libraries in the United States. These ideas were far from neutral. A good place to start is with Sidney Ditzion's *Arsenals of a Democratic Culture: A Social History of the American Public Library Movement in New England and the Middle States from 1850 to 1900* of 1947. The title sets the tone, and the text begins by quoting President Roosevelt:

> In our country's first year of war, we have seen the growing power of books as weapons. . . . This is proper, for a war of ideas can no more be won without books than a naval war can be won without ships. . . . Libraries are directly and immediately involved in the conflict which divides our world, and for two reasons; first, because they are essential for the functioning and democratic society; second because the contemporary conflict touches the integrity of scholarship, the freedom of the mind, and even the survival of culture, and libraries are the great tools of scholarship, the great repositories of culture, and the great symbols of the freedom of the mind.[1]

As Ditzion shows, multiple ideas have influenced the development of public libraries in the United States. One is economic: that continued industrial and commercial prosperity depended on an educated populace. The English economist Stanley Jevons, for example, had argued that even if free libraries were very costly, they would be less expensive than prisons, poorhouses, and other institutions maintained by public money, or the gin palaces, music halls, and theaters maintained by private expenditures.[2] The formal education provided in schools was unlikely to be adequate for industrial and commercial needs, especially when labor was relatively scarce. Immigrants would need remedial educational help. These reasons indicated why any institution that could foster literacy and assist adult education was valuable. Public libraries supported both. As a new industrial working class emerged, an industrial argument surfaced. Samuel Gompers, the trade unionist leader, wrote in 1897, "The rendezvous of labor, when unorganized, is usually the saloon; when organized it is transferred to the meeting room, the club room or library."[3]

Political considerations arose. One was that if libraries were truly to serve the public at large, then they should be controlled by the public and funded by the public. This meant that subscription libraries should become or be replaced by *public* libraries, which meant that they should be provided by the people (through local government), funded by the people (using tax revenues), and be free for the public to use. As Jevons wrote, libraries "are classed with town halls, police courts, prisons, and poorhouses as necessary adjuncts of our stage of civilization."[4]

Another political idea related to republicanism. If the United States, both individually and federally, were to remain a republic, then citizens needed sufficient knowledge to support their electoral role effectively. Associated with republicanism was the notion of individual worth, the need for the dissemination of useful knowledge, and self-fulfillment. Ditzion refers to this as a kind of cultural nationalism: "The new culture, exhibiting an exuberance of movement, expansion, progress and participation, celebrating individualism, local independence and initiative, and exalting the humane spirit, molded the democratic faith into a religion of nationalism."[5]

Democracy and republicanism implied a culture of equality, and "The free library was to be an intellectual and literary common where the humblest and the highest would meet on equal terms as they did at the polls."[6] Further, "the strongest threats to democracy were understood to be from ignorant classes who would vote for the wrong parties either because of their own untutored choice or because of the scheming leadership of city politicians. America would be the victim of its own humane spirit if it did not educate and inform its 'illiterate blacks and foreign born.'"[7] Political evolution was to be preferred to political revolution, and foreign-born readers needed to be Americanized.

The library was seen as an educational institution, a kind of superstructure that could continue and remedy any deficiencies of the school system, even provide instruction through amusement. Civic enlightenment and personal development have remained constant objectives of the American public library. Initially, the collection of library books was the primary concern, but the provision of materials progressively was augmented by personal assistance, stimulation and outreach, and service designed for specific groups. Moral betterment was emphasized from around 1850 to 1890, vocational improvement was a major goal during the years between 1930 and 1950, and community development was a major concern after that.[8]

Individualism and personal responsibility for self-development had very deep roots in U.S. culture. Renaissance attention to the individual, Protestant emphasis on direct engagement with the Bible and personal responsibility for good works and salvation, Enlightenment emphasis on reason, and Romantic concern for the individual spirit all fed democratic theory in the United States.

In addition, a charitable, humanitarian mission reflected, as one speaker put it in 1866, "the responsibility of the gifted and educated classes toward the weak, the witless, and the ignorant."[9] Like the YMCA, the public library offered wholesome options, self-help, and visions of a better world. The public library fitted the U.S. habit of philanthropic support for socially beneficial initiatives. Andrew Carnegie was famous for his outstanding financial aid. The usual agreement was that Carnegie would pay for a library building if the local community undertook to sustain library service. He said:

> There is not such a cradle of pure democracy upon the earth as in the Free Public Library, this republic of letters where neither rank, office nor wealth receives the slightest consideration, where all men are equal. More than this, here in many instances, the poor man having more knowledge of books than the noble or millionaire is the larger partner in the library.[10]

Carnegie was the most prominent figure within a well-developed custom of philanthropy that was, and remains, much less marked in other countries.[11]

Ditzion provided the most widely accepted account of the rise of the public library in the United States. Other historians have differed in their emphases.[12] A gendered view of libraries and librarians emerged associated with the perception of libraries—especially public and school libraries—as nurturing, and library service as an occupation for women in the United States.[13] Another view emphasized the role of class and argued that American public libraries were agents of social control exercised by members of the upper classes who sought to influence the behavior of the masses that frequented public libraries.[14]

The migration from rural to urban living, concern to raise the socioeconomic status of the worker, and the steady increase in publications favored the development of public libraries. With the rise of the cult of efficiency, the technical development and professional status of library science emerged with professional education provided in technical colleges and universities as well as in a few large libraries.

The ideas about public libraries were part of a broader view. An active local public library depended on the idea that local government *should* be allowed, even encouraged, to develop local services. Philanthropic support for libraries was one aspect of a broader favorable view that philanthropy could and should supplement governmental activities. In other words, free public libraries depended on a set of ideas about how society should function. Free public libraries would not have emerged in the absence of a social and political consensus supportive of conditions within which public libraries could thrive.

Social historian Merle Curti considered the American public library "one of the most characteristically American of our major cultural institutions."[15] It can be said that these ideas were not fully reflected in reality. Notably, racism caused failures "to educate and inform its 'illiterate blacks and foreign born.'" Nevertheless, all of these ideas were influential.

COMPARISON

A difficulty with the explanations of the ideology of U.S. public libraries by Ditzion and others is that although the explanations differed, all more or less converged in being supportive of the development of public libraries, with little basis for knowing their relative importance. Further, a descriptive examination of a single country provides limited insight. One way to gain more insight would be to compare different countries. As one example, if liberal democratic aspirations were a powerful force for public libraries in the United States, what about public library development in countries that were not democratic or not liberal? Lenin and his librarian wife, Nadezhda Krupskaya, for example, strongly supported public libraries in the Soviet Union, but not for Western liberal democracy.

During the 1960s and 1970s, numerous studies of library services of different countries were implicitly or explicitly comparative. The limitation was that they were heavily descriptive with very little attention to explanatory analysis. Since then, the tendency has been the opposite: to start with an explanatory analysis, relating to, perhaps, colonialism, gender, or Marxist analysis, and to project that perspective onto some situation as a preselected lens for interpretation. This has different limitations. For our purposes, we draw on an exemplary comparative analysis of the development of public libraries in the United States, Great Britain, and France from 1850 to 1914 by Jean Hassenforder.[16]

PUBLIC LIBRARIES IN FRANCE

In the mid-nineteenth century France, Great Britain, and the United States were three of the leading world powers and more modern in several ways than the Habsburg and Russian Empires. Germany and Italy did not yet exist as nation-states. France, Britain, and the United States were increasingly democratic, experiencing the industrial revolution, rapid technological development, and urbanization. They shared a western European cultural heritage. They had much in common. Each was well-informed about the other two, and they influenced each other. Yet library development, especially public library development, differed radically in France from the United States and the Britain.[17]

The U.S. constitution defines a federation of individual states that were and have remained eager to maintain as much autonomy as they can. Within each state, local government is strong, as it always has been in Great Britain. In North America large distances and transportation delays, in any case, would have made centralized control impractical. In France, by contrast, the nation-state had emerged very gradually from a medieval quilt of very varied jurisdictions and local customs. Henri IV achieved political unity in 1604; and Louis XIV, king from 1643 to 1715, systematically concentrated power in his central government. The French Revolution swept away all of the existing regional and local political structures and installed an entirely new and centrally controlled system of local government units ("departments") with new geographical boundaries. But French local government had limited autonomy because the central government in the capital, Paris, exercised an influence and control that would have been unimaginable in the United States.

In the United States, as in Great Britain, the emerging municipal libraries were new institutions intended for all of the population. They were seen as active agencies for the improvement of society, providing support for individual self-help. The people in charge were able to innovate, and these new institutions could evolve freely. They had good models to draw on in the form of subscription libraries and working men's societies.

In France, the situation was very different. Municipal libraries already existed, but these were small collections of ancient books confiscated from nobles in the eighteenth century. Cities were mandated to preserve them, but cities had little interest in spending money for good storage, competent staffing, or adding new materials. So, these fossilized non-lending collections were not developed and were of interest to only a few local scholars. Separately, France had small popular libraries. These were small collections of books that could be borrowed. No reading area was provided, and opening hours and budgets were very limited. The Ministry of Education also mandated school libraries. Like the popular libraries, these were, separately, small, neglected lending collections. As a result, the ecological niche in which the new free public libraries could blossom in Great Britain and the United States already was occupied in France by three separate, very limited operations, composed of very small collections and minimal staffing, access, or support. The few individuals associated with these services had a vested interest in them. The emphasis on local government autonomy and the philanthropic support so influential in the United States were absent.

In France, the distinction was clear-cut between the popular libraries for the general public and the municipal libraries that the scholarly élite frequented. In the latter, concern for preservation inhibited concern for contemporary needs. The first American-style free public library service and a bookmobile were provided independent of official channels by a wartime relief organization. The American Committee for Devastated France (in French, Comité américain pour les régions dévastées [CARD]) was active at the western front from 1917 to 1924—staffed by U.S. volunteers, funded by U.S. philanthropy, and led by a Canadian doctor, Anne Murray Dike, and heiress Anne Tracy Morgan. CARD provided emergency relief and, then, increasingly, community building, with library services led by Jessie Carson, a children's librarian from the New York Public Library.[18]

Some research libraries in France were large, but little service was provided. The emphasis in both municipal and research libraries was famously on conservation, not communication. The national library was among the largest in the world but was notoriously conservative until a politically active documentalist, Julien Cain, was appointed director in 1930 with a charge to modernize it. Even basic, useful reference works had been kept in closed stacks until 1934 when, at Cain's direction, Suzanne Briet opened a well-stocked and staffed reference and bibliography room.

This situation saw scholarly study of old books and manuscripts, at least in the larger research libraries, but no opportunity and no preparation for implementing the new styles of library service emerging in the United States. The only school where training for librarianship was provided was the Ecole des Chartes ("School of Charters"), founded to prepare archivists to conserve the collections of medieval charters and other manuscripts confiscated during the French Revolution. The curriculum was based on the techniques historians used then, notably philology (the interpretation of old texts) and paleography (the deciphering of old handwriting). Eventually, minimal instruction in librarianship gradually was added. The staffing of French research libraries was dominated by graduates of this program. They were called "conservators." The situation was so bad that the American Library Association, in collaboration with American philanthropists and members of the French library community, established an independent American-style library school in Paris that operated from 1924 to 1929 and had a highly stimulating effect.[19] The role of foreign intervention in library services will be examined further in chapter 5.

Ideas about education also were quite different in France. Education was highly standardized and regimented, and the public schools were tightly controlled from Paris. Famously, if you were to name a child in any grade in any school, the minister of education could immediately tell you what topic that child was being taught at that moment. Nationally, the emphasis was on passing exams, competing to attend elite schools, and obtaining the right diplomas. Far less respect was accorded the self-taught or self-improvement outside the formal education system that was so prevalent in the United States, let alone the English cult of the expert amateur.

The United States was a diverse country; France was a divided one, with deep political, religious, and social divisions. In this climate, attempts at reform ran into opposition. In the United States, a variety of political, legal, religious, and other cultural factors converged to support the development of free public libraries. Hassenforder's detailed analysis reveals how in France political, legal, religious, and other cultural factors reinforced each other in impeding the development of public library services. Leading librarians in France were aware of the difference but were not in a position to effect changes. Some, notably Eugène Morel and Maurice Pellisson, campaigned for improvement by drawing attention to the more developed library services elsewhere, primarily in Great Britain and the United States.

In 1908, seeking good examples worldwide, Morel commended recent developments in Japan: "In debt from the prodigious effort of its [military] victory, Japan has nevertheless not forgotten the sources of her victory, she buys cannons and she buys books."[20]

Pellisson, in 1906, noted library development efforts in California, he wrote, by "activists full of zeal."[21] Our next chapter takes us to California to see what Pellisson admired. The development of library services in rural areas there is a noteworthy story and, as we will see, it later inspired initiatives in Japan and elsewhere.

NOTES

1. Sidney Herbert Ditzion, *Arsenals of a Democratic Culture: A Social History of the American Public Library Movement in New England and the Middle States from 1850 to 1900* (Chicago: American Library Association, 1947), vi.

2. Stanley Jevons, "The Rationale of Free Public Libraries," *Contemporary Review* 16, no. 3 (March 1881): 385–402. Reprinted in David Gerard, ed., *Libraries in Society: A Reader* (London: Bingley, 1978), 16–20.

3. Ditzion, *Arsenals*, 126.

4. Jevons, "Rationale," 387.

5. Ditzion, *Arsenals*, 57.

6. Ditzion, *Arsenals*, 60.

7. Ditzion, *Arsenals*, 65.

8. Robert Ellis Lee, *Continuing Education for Adults through the American Public Library, 1833–1964* (Chicago, American Library Association, 1966).

9. Ditzion, *Arsenals*, 97.

10. Ditzion, *Arsenals*, 154.

11. As of February 2020, up to 60 percent of personal income in the United States is exempted from income tax if donated to charitable organizations, which, in turn, largely are exempt from corporate taxes.

12. Good overviews of the differing explanations are provided by Francis Miksa, "The Interpretation of American Public Library History," 73–92, in *Public Librarianship: A Reader*, edited by Jane Robbins Carter (Littleton, CO: Libraries Unlimited, 1982); and Robert V. Williams, "The Public Library as the Dependent Variable: Historically Oriented Theories and Hypotheses of Public Library Development," *Journal of Library History* 16, no. 2 (Spring 1981): 329–41. See also Rosemary R. Du Mont, *Reform and Reaction: The Big City Public Library in American Life* (Westport, CT: Greenwood, 1977); Dee Garrison, *Apostles of Culture: The Public Librarian and American Society, 1876–1920* (New York: Free Press, 1979); Michael Harris, "The Purpose of the American Public Library: A Revisionist Interpretation of History," *Library Journal* 98 (September 15, 1973): 2509–14; Lee, *Continuing Education for Adults*; Lowell Martin, *Enlightenment: A History of the Public Library in the United States in the Twentieth Century* (Lanham, MD: Scarecrow, 1998); Douglas Raber, *Librarianship and Legitimacy: The Ideology of the Public Library* (Westport, CT: Greenwood, 1997); Jesse H. Shera, *Foundations of the Public Library: The Origins of the Public Library Movement in New England, 1629–1855* (Chicago: University of Chicago Press, 1944); Wayne A. Wiegand, *Part of Our Lives: A People's History of the American Public Library* (New York: Oxford University Press, 2015); and Patrick Williams, *The American Public Library and the Problem of Purpose* (New York: Greenwood, 1988).

13. Garrison, *Apostles*.

14. Argued especially by Michael Harris; for example, Harris, "Purpose of the American Public Library."

15. Ditzion, *Arsenals*, vii.

16. Jean Hassenforder, *Développement comparé des bibliothèques publiques en France, en Grande-Bretagne et aux États-Unis dans la seconde moitié du XIXe siècle (1850–1914)* (Paris: Cercle de la librairie, 1967). A brief summary in English is in his "Comparative studies and the

development of libraries," *UNESCO Bulletin for Libraries* 22, no. 1 (1968): 13–19. For the history of libraries in France, see *Histoire des bibliothèques françaises*, edited by André Vernet and others, 4 vols. (Paris: Promodis-Editions du Cercle du librairie, 1988–1992).

17. This section is based on Hassenforder, *Développement*.

18. Marcelline Dormont, "The French Connection: Remembering the American Librarians of Post-WWI France," *American Libraries* (February 16, 2017), https://americanlibrariesmagazine.org/2017/02/16/french-connection-librarians-wwi-france/.

19. Dormont, "The French Connection." For librarianship in France between the two world wars, see Sylvie Fayet-Scribe, "Women Professionals in France during the 1930s," *Libraries and the Cultural Record* 44, no. 2 (2009): 201–19.

20. Eugène Morel, Bibliothèques, essai sur le développement des bibliothèques publiques et de la librairie dans les deux mondes, vol. 1 (Paris: Mercure de France, 1908–1909), http://catalog.hathitrust.org/Record/001164300.

21. Maurice Pellisson, *Les bibliothèques populairs à l'étranger et en France* (Paris: Imprimerie Nationale, 1906), 27; also, https://catalog.hathitrust.org/Record/000961498, "On vit que les États du Nord et de l'Est ont une singulière avance sur ceux de l'Ouest et du Sud. Mais, dans ces dernières années, les retardataires se sont mis en movement à leur tour; en California, dans le Mississipi en particulier, la cause des bibliothèques publiques a trouvé des partisans pleins de zèle et l'écart que nous signalons ne tardera pas à diminuer."

Chapter Four

The California County Library System

> The California county libraries are much more than mere local units administered by their respective counties . . . they constitute a unified system of library service. —Carleton Joeckel, 1935

Immediately upon statehood in 1850, California had established and ambitiously developed a State Library. By the end of the nineteenth century, it had the second largest collection of the state libraries in the United States, with one hundred thousand items. Only the New York's State Library collection was larger. Service, however, was less well developed. Only state employees and legislators and their staff were permitted to use the library. Appointments to the library staff were not based on merit or qualifications but used as political patronage.

At 163,696 square miles (423,970 km^2) and a population of one and a half million in 1900, California was a large state and mostly rural. Legislation authorized cities to provide a public library, but counties, the local government unit responsible for rural areas outside cities, were not legally authorized to provide library services. So public library service was absent outside of a few towns.

City libraries were few and mostly recent. Berkeley, for example, the home of the University of California since 1873, had no public library service until 1893 when 264 donated volumes were made available. In 1905, a public library building, funded by Andrew Carnegie, was opened on the site of a garden donated for the purpose by Rosa Shattuck, a leading citizen. The city's population then grew rapidly with refugees from the great earthquake and fire of San Francisco in 1906.

As of 1900, no professional education programs were available for librarians in California or any of the other Western states. Nevertheless, California was exceptional for the speed with which quality rural public library services were developed through what became known as the California County Library System.

JAMES GILLIS

The California County Library System originated with an epiphany by James Louis Gillis (1857–1917), a railroad manager who became a librarian. It is a heroic tale vividly told by two women who were actively involved: a melodramatic account, *The Beginning and the End of the Best Library Service in the World*, by Laura Steffens Suggett, in 1924; and a later, more matter-of-fact account in Harriet G. Eddy's *County Free Library Organizing in California, 1909–1918*, in 1955.[1]

At age four, James Gillis was brought seventeen hundred miles west from Iowa by ox cart, crossing the Sierra Nevada mountain chain. He became a messenger boy for the Sacramento Valley Railroad Company, a division of the Southern Pacific railroad system, based in Sacramento. After rising through the ranks to become assistant superintendent, he decided to leave the railroad after a particularly violent labor dispute in which strikers died. Sacramento was the state capital of California, and in 1894 he moved to a quieter life in state bureaucracy. He worked for the State Assembly as chief clerk to the legislature's ways and means committee and as keeper of the archives of the secretary of state. In the course of his work, he would use the California State Library.

One day when Gillis visited the State Library, it was empty. No readers or staff were to be seen. He looked around and had an inspiring thought: what an engine for social progress this institution could be if only it were directed in the right way! A colleague later wrote of this episode:

> It required a man with the most vivid imagination to be able to walk into the rotunda of the California State Library one day back in 1898 and finding it utterly unattended, to say, "How I'd like to show them how to run this institution!" ... When he looked around that empty rotunda, he saw, as he himself once told me, a combination of conditions that, united, could bring to California a library service second to none: first he saw this splendid plant, supplied with the stock to operate it but no medium to put it into use; second, he saw the people out all over the state, the people he knew and the state he loved so well, wanting and needing this library supply now locked against them; and finally he sensed the need of a distributing agency that would unlock these books and take them to the people.[2]

Because State Library appointments were political patronage, Gillis was able to arrange to be appointed deputy state librarian in 1898 and state librarian the next year. He then changed the rules so that all future staff appointments within the State Library had to be made on merit, not through patronage.

Figure 4.1. James Gillis.

After a tour inspecting library services in the Midwest and eastern states, he set out to develop a system of public library services for California. He followed the lead of the State Library of Wisconsin where a research and information service for the state legislature had been highly developed, even to the extent of drafting legislation, by an enterprising state librarian, Charles McCarthy.[3] Gillis worked with progressive librarians and helped to develop the California Library Association, but it took time to get legislation passed authorizing counties to provide free public library services. As an interim step, cities were authorized to serve rural areas under contract.

Gillis's first plan was to set up a department in 1903 to provide a system of collections of books deposited in localities lacking a public library. These were placed almost anywhere someone would take responsibility for them. By 1906, two hundred such "traveling libraries" each averaged fifty carefully selected volumes.[4] It was, however, a cumbersome and ineffective service. What was really needed was a library service provided locally by the local government, but the counties responsible for most of California were not authorized to do that. It would require enabling legislation authorizing counties to provide library services and then inducing them to do so.

LIBRARY SERVICE

Modern management techniques had been pioneered largely by railroad companies to cope with the complexities they faced as they expanded their networks and needed to interoperate with other companies. Gillis's appointment as state librarian came at a time when scientific management, pioneered by Frederick W. Taylor and others, had become highly influential. Scientific management and the use of efficiency experts eventually were regarded as tools to enable capitalist enterprises to exploit employees, but in Gillis's time they still were viewed positively by workers and unions as well as by managers. The reason was that if more efficient methods could yield greater productivity with the same investment of labor and capital, then the benefit of that additional yield could be shared. This shared benefit and avoidance of waste were even seen as peaceful alternatives to the zero-sum game of class conflict. So, efficiency was not only progressive but even a moral imperative, much as recycling is today. The cult of efficiency was embraced by all kinds of professions worldwide and promoted vigorously among librarians by Melvil Dewey.[5]

After learning from Wisconsin and elsewhere, Gillis initiated a wide-ranging series of reforms and innovations. A new general reading room was created and opened to all. A catalog of the library's collection was completed, and a bulletin of new accessions produced and published. Knowing which libraries held which titles enabled libraries to borrow from each other when needed, so the first "union catalog" in the United States was undertaken to record the holdings of other libraries in the state. In this way, all libraries' collections could be shared as one vast virtual collection. The State Library paid for interlibrary loan delivery and undertook to supply copies of needed books not in any county library, buying a copy if need be. To support reference service, the indexing of California newspapers was initiated. Other libraries could forward difficult reference questions to the State Library reference service for an answer.

New departments were created. A California history department was established to collect and preserve material relating to the state and its history. The nation's first department of books for the blind and visually impaired was formed. A department of sociology was created to study what information would be needed to support legislation and, following Wisconsin's lead, a legislative information service was created for legislators in the state senate and assembly. Book selection became more focused on California and the needs of state government and the legislature rather than continuing to build a large general collection that would duplicate the collections of California's growing university libraries.

In this way a well-designed and mutually beneficial system was developed, a triumph of progressive thinking and efficiency.[6] Although it was not the first system of county library services, it soon was regarded as exemplary.

HARRIET EDDY

State Librarian Gillis encountered difficulties getting the approval of satisfactory legislation to authorize county library services. As an interim measure, legislation was enacted that allowed a city to contract to provide library service in rural areas outside its boundaries. The first such contract resulted from an initiative by Harriet Eddy.

Harriet Gertrude Eddy (1876–1966) grew up in Michigan. In college she won a prize for excellence in biblical Greek. She then taught Latin in a secondary school. After some graduate study in Latin and English at the University of Chicago, she traveled in Europe. On her return she taught Latin and English in Montana before joining her sister in Elk Grove, California, where she became principal of the secondary school.[7] One of the State Library's small "traveling library" collections of books was housed in Eddy's school, but for her school to become accredited, it needed a better library, so she wrote to the state librarian asking for more books. Gillis, who wanted to see implementation of the legislation allowing cities to provide library service in county areas under contract, arranged for the nearby Sacramento

Figure 4.2. Harriet Eddy, 1902.

Public Library to provide Oak Grove with a larger collection under Eddy's supervision.

Eddy vigorously promoted use of the books entrusted to her, and she engaged her students in this. If they learned that a local farmer was trying a new crop or had an unproductive fruit tree, Eddy and her students would find a suitable book on the topic and take it to the farmer. After learning about her vigorous outreach, Gillis persuaded Eddy to attend a meeting of the California Library Association to tell librarians about her use of the collection. She did. Gillis then persuaded her to resign her position as school principal and go to work with him at the State Library. Her role would be "extension," promoting the development of library services outside the State Library.

A small library cannot provide sophisticated library service: the collection is too small, and it cannot afford specialized staff. Service capability depends on scale. Gillis judged that a single library system serving an entire county, even excluding cities that preferred to provide library service independently, would be large enough to provide good public library service and would have the advantage of fitting the existing local government structure. He preferred that responsibility for public library service be directly under a county's governing body, the Board of Supervisors, and kept separate from the provision of schools by the county board of education.

After approval of legislation authorizing counties to provide free library service, Gillis charged Eddy to stir up public demand and to persuade county governments to start providing service. Sydney Mitchell, founding director of the Berkeley School of Librarianship, wrote of her, "She was an extraordinary person. . . . she was a spellbinder! She could have been an evangelist, or a salesman, or any of those things, and her job was to go around to the women's organizations, even the men's supervisors meetings, and simply talk them into assessing taxes and establishing a county library."[8]

THE CALIFORNIA COUNTY LIBRARY SYSTEM

The system developed under Gillis's leadership was a well-designed package with the following components:

- The county library law of 1911 authorized but did not require county boards of supervisors to provide public library services in unserved areas and to assess taxes for the purpose.
- Towns with tax-supported libraries were excluded but could join the county service.
- Counties with small populations could combine.
- Service must be free. No fees were allowed for using the library or borrowing books.
- The director of a county library must be certified to be professionally qualified by an examining board administered by the state librarian.
- The State Library employed specialists to provide technical guidance.

- When a reader needed a book that the county library did not have, the State Library would supply it from its own holdings, obtain it through its union catalog, or, if need be, buy it.
- Some state funding for books for teachers was reallocated to free county library service.

The State Library reprogrammed its own budget to reflect its changed strategic priorities. Collection development became more narrowly focused on materials relating to California and its needs. Staffing increasingly was directed toward fostering the development of other libraries. The need to sustain the development of a large general collection could now be left to the rapidly growing libraries at the University of California, Stanford University, and the University of Southern California.

Harriet Eddy and her colleagues had effective political skills. When they first went to a county to advocate for free county library service, they would begin by visiting each member of the county's board of supervisors in his home. This ensured that he would be among the first to know and best informed about what was being proposed, and they might be able to enlist the support of the supervisor's spouse. They then would systematically start talking to women's clubs and many other organizations, and visit other leading politicians in their homes. When they thought that they had enough support, they would organize a petition to the board of supervisors and marshal all of the endorsements they could. It worked. Within about four years, forty of forty-six counties had initiated free county library service, each coordinated with the State Library and, through its union catalog, with other libraries in California. An invigorated California Library Association helped.

Carleton Joeckel, the Berkeley city librarian, later wrote in his authoritative treatise on public library governance that the California system was "outstanding":

> The California county libraries are much more than mere local units administered by their respective counties. More nearly, perhaps, than any other group of American libraries, they constitute a unified system of library service, and this aspect of their situation should be emphasized. The state maintains a very considerable amount of control through the "general supervision" of the county library system by the state librarian, which is provided by the law. In the second place, all county librarians must be certificated under examinations conducted by the Board of Library Examiners, of which the state librarian is chairman. In making appointments the county supervisors must confine their selections to persons on the eligible list thus established. . . . On the whole, then, the picture is that of a library system centering in the state library. Local autonomy is not eliminated, but the influence of the state is very important. The county librarian is a powerful administrative officer who looks to the county for support but also looks to the state as the fountainhead of the system.[9]

The California county library system was widely admired. It was regarded as an example for others to follow. William S. Learned's inspirational tract *The American Public Library and the Diffusion of Knowledge*, published in 1924, included an enthusiastic account of the California county library system, "considered by students of library problems the country over to be the ideal type of organization for rural and small urban book service."[10] Alvin Johnson's *The Public Library—A People's University* (1938) singled out the California county library system for praise.[11] Officials in the Soviet Union surveyed the development of library services in other countries and identified the California county library system as exemplary. In 1927 Eddy was invited to the Soviet Union to explain it and to discuss its applicability in Russia. She returned in 1930–1931.[12] Gillis's successor as state librarian, Milton S. Ferguson, drew on California's experience when he and Septimus Pitt, the Glasgow city librarian, conducted a detailed survey of conditions in South Africa and made influential recommendations for library development.[13]

TRAINING LIBRARIANS

In the absence of a school of librarianship in any of the Western states at the beginning of the twentieth century, the shortage of qualified librarians was acute. Repeated attempts to start a program at the University of California in Berkeley were blocked by Benjamin Ide Wheeler, the university's autocratic president. In frustration Gillis eventually started his own school at the State Library pending progress at Berkeley.[14]

At Berkeley, Joseph Rowell, the long-time university librarian, had lost interest in managing the library and had delegated administrative duties to his deputy, Harold Leupp. When the United States entered the European War in 1917, Leupp joined the army, and so responsibility for managing the library was assigned to Sydney Mitchell, the associate university librarian.

Sydney Bancroft Mitchell (1878–1951) was a shrewd Canadian immigrant from Quebec, and he was greatly concerned about the need to train more librarians. He learned that during the war, administrative procedures had become more relaxed and that the dean of the College of Letters and Science had the authority to approve individual courses. So, Mitchell and Edith Coulter, the head reference librarian, designed a list of courses on librarianship and quietly had the dean approve them. These courses were listed to the 1918–1919 campus catalog of courses, and library staff, with the help of local librarians, started teaching these courses in the Fall semester of 1918 to students who already were enrolled on campus. President Wheeler was unaware of this activity until after the first cohort of students had completed the year-long program. Fortunately, when he found out, he agreed to allow the program to continue, and a formal certificate was approved to confer on subsequent students completing the program. A department of library science was established within the College of Letters and Science to administer it, and a budget gradually was provided.

Gillis died unexpectedly in 1917. His successor as state librarian, Milton Ferguson, was content to discontinue the California State Library School after Mitchell assured him that attention would be paid to county library service in the Berkeley program. The school's limited curriculum did have an emphasis on public libraries, especially county library service, and the State Library helped by assigning staff as part-time instructors. The school's *Announcement* for 1926–1927 lists a course, "The American Public Library," taught by Carleton Joeckel, Berkeley's city librarian, who became the leading authority on public library governance. "County Library Law" was taught by May Dexter Henshall, a library organizer at the State Library, and "County Library Administration" was taught by Mary Barmby, the Alameda County librarian. Like almost all directors of such schools until late in the twentieth century, Mitchell came to that role from a career in library administration, and he specialized in problems of library management.

In California in the early twentieth century, public library service was seen as important for advancing educational, personal, economic, social, and political progress. Public libraries were more closely associated with adult education then than now. The library collections, reference works, and librarians eager to advise could complement the regimented school system by providing individualized, educational self-help at the level, pace, and time convenient for the reader. More generally, open access to well-chosen collections in a free public library empowered the individual to achieve his own personal potential within a culture that favored personal liberty and social mobility. Educational self-help fostered a better-educated workforce. Access to the latest commercial and technical ideas facilitated efficiency and progress in industry, agriculture, and all other spheres of life.

The power and importance of good public library service as a social and political force in supporting Western liberal democracy was not in doubt. In November 1938, shortly after Hitler had invaded Czechoslovakia, and Nazi Germany, Fascist Italy, and militaristic Japan increasingly were seen as threatening, Sydney Mitchell, then president of the California Library Association, gave a powerful and eloquent address on "the public library in the defense of democracy."[15] He noted that whereas school, college, and university libraries had to advance the objectives and policies of their institutions, public libraries were comparatively free to determine their own policies. Democracy he defined as "a way of life where the dignity and freedom of the individual are conserved, as contrasted with life in the totalitarian state, which subordinates the individual and requires conformity to the dominant ideas." He continued:

Librarians should be all for democracy, as under no other system of government now in effect can the public library, as we understand it, persist. In the totalitarian state the librarian becomes merely an agency for propaganda, for the dissemination of such information as the authorities care to pass on.

Mitchell then reviewed dangers to democracy, always with library-related examples. He starting with intolerance, noting racial intolerance and mentioning examples of discrimination in library employment he had encountered. He denounced intolerance of ideas, including religious and political prejudice in society and in book selection. A second danger to democracy was failure of social groups to understand each other, which could be mitigated by attentive library collection development. A third danger was lack of critical thinking. The public library should do what it can to spread "the proper skepticism of panaceas." Next, he urged that the membership of the boards responsible for supervising public libraries have greater diversity and be more representative of their communities. "Library schools," he said, "are now quite properly being asked to furnish young men and women of initiative and social consciousness, not gentle readers and introverts." That requires merit-based appointments and protection of individuals through staff organizations. Finally, "let me say that it is the hard things which I have found most interesting, most stimulating."

The California county library system was a service designed by a community for its own cultural and political needs. The next chapter examines the different case of library service provided by or from one country to exert cultural and political influence in another different country.

NOTES

1. Laura Steffens Suggett, *The Beginning and the End of the Best Library Service in the World* (San Francisco: San Francisco Publishing Co., 1924); Harriet G. Eddy, *County Free Library Organizing in California, 1909–1918* (Sacramento: California Library Association, 1955). See also Ray E. Held, *The Rise of the Public Library in California* (Chicago: American Library Association, 1973); and May Dexter Henshall, "California County Free Library," *Library Journal* 54, no. 14 (August 1929): 643–46. For Gillis, see the special issue on him "James Gillis" in *News Notes of California Libraries* 52, no. 4 (October 1957): 633–714; also, Kathleen Correia and John Gonzales, "Biographies of State Librarians from 1850 to the Present," *California State Library Foundation Bulletin*, 68 (Spring/Summer 2000): 1–18; Theodora R. Brewitt, "James L. Gillis 1857–1917," 74–84, in *Pioneering Leaders in Librarianship*, edited by Emily M. Danton (Chicago: American Library Association, 1953). Debra G. Hansen, "Depoliticizing the California State Library: The Political and Professional Transformation of James Gillis, 1890–1917," *Information and Culture* 48, no. 1 (2013): 68–90; and Ray E. Held, "Gillis, James Louis (1957–1917)," 197–200, in *Dictionary of American Library Biography*, edited by Bohdan S. Wynar (Littleton, CO: Libraries Unlimited, 1978).

2. Harriet G. Eddy, [Comments on James Gillis], *News Notes of California Libraries* 52, no. 4 (October 1957): 712.

3. Marion Casey, *Charles McCarthy: Librarianship and Reform* (Chicago: American Library Association, 1981).

4. *News Notes of California Libraries* published by the California State Library from 1906 is an excellent source for library developments in California. For an annotated list of the books in each of three such traveling libraries, see California State Library and James L. Gillis, *Descriptive List of the Libraries of California* (Sacramento: W. W. Shannon, superintendent of State Printing, 1904), 97–116.

5. Samuel Haber, *Efficiency and Uplift: Scientific Management in the Progressive Era, 1890–1920* (Chicago; University of Chicago Press, 1964).

6. For examples of Gillis's writings, see "Relation of State Libraries to other Educational Institutions," National Association of State Libraries. *Proceedings and Addresses, Eleventh Convention* (1908): 29–30; and "Shall the State Library be Head of All Library Activities in the State," National Association of State Libraries. *Proceedings and Addresses, Fourteenth Convention* (1911): 12–13.

7. For Eddy, see John V. Richardson, "Harriet G. Eddy (1876–1966): California's First County Library Organizer and her Influence on USSR Libraries," *California State Library Foundation Bulletin*, 94 (2009): 2–13, http://www.cslfdn.org/pdf/Issue94.pdf; and Marion S. Wachtel, "Harriet G. Eddy," *California Librarian* 28, no. 1 (January 1967): 54–55.

8. Mitchell had a parallel career in adapting East Coast plant-breeding practices to the West Coast climate. He was a founder and longtime president of the California Horticultural Society, bred irises, and wrote best-selling gardening books and a popular column in *Sunset Magazine*. The citation for his honorary doctorate from Occidental College stated, "Thus he has the dual facility of making people more fruitful and flowers more beautiful." See Sydney B. Mitchell, *Mitchell of California: Memoirs of Sydney B. Mitchell Librarian, Teacher, Gardener* (Berkeley: California Library Association, 1960), 216–17; and Robert Brundin, "Sydney Bancroft Mitchell and the Establishment of the Graduate School of Librarianship," *Libraries & Culture* 29, no. 2 (1994): 166–85.

9. Carleton B. Joeckel, *The Government of the American Public Library* (Chicago: University of Chicago Press, 1935), 268.

10. William S. Learned, *The American Public Library and the Diffusion of Knowledge* (New York: Harcourt, Brace, 1924), 55.

11. Alvin S. Johnson, *The Public Library: A People's University* (New York: American Association for Adult Education, 1938).

12. Richardson, "Harriet G. Eddy."

13. Milton James Ferguson, *Memorandum: Libraries in the Union of South Africa, Rhodesia and Kenya Colony* (New York: Carnegie Corp., 1929), http://catalog.hathitrust.org/Record/001165635.

14. Beulah Mumm, "California State Library School," *News Notes of California Libraries* 52, no. 4 (October 1957): 679–82.

15. Sydney Mitchell, "The Public Library in the Defense of Democracy," *Library Journal* 64, no. 6 (March 15, 1939): 209–12.

Chapter Five

Libraries in Cultural Diplomacy

> In our country's first year of war, we have seen the growing power of books as weapons. . . . This is proper, for a war of ideas can no more be won without books than a naval war can be won without ships. —Franklin D. Roosevelt [1]

Foreign policy, like military strategy, is the art of inducing desired behavior in or by other countries. Foreign policy usually is thought of in terms of negotiation and treaties, but it also includes the use of cultural activities to promote desired behavior. In its crudest form, this is simply propaganda. In a subtler form, it includes cultural engagement using radio broadcasts, language classes, exhibits, student exchanges, and other initiatives to promote understanding and sympathy.

Japan, for example, used radio broadcasts. In 1944 the Broadcasting Corporation of Japan was exporting radio broadcasts in twenty-six languages and dialects, with fifty-nine daily overseas programs in the English language alone, including popular music programs targeted at U.S. troops by the mythical "Tokyo Rose." [2]

In Western democracies' dealings with underdeveloped and totalitarian regimes, outreach included the provision of libraries and information centers to disseminate information reflecting favorably on their own policies and encourage democratic ideas, especially among opinion leaders, such as journalists, intellectuals, and politicians, in the targeted countries. [3]

GEORGE CREEL AND THE COMMITTEE ON PUBLIC INFORMATION

The U.S. government experimented with cultural diplomacy during World War I. In April 1917 President Woodrow Wilson appointed George Creel, a journalist, reformer, and political campaigner, chairman of a Committee on Public Information. Creel engaged with astonishing energy. "It was in this recognition of Public Opinion as a major force that the Great War differed most essentially from all previous conflicts," he later wrote, and ". . . German *Kultur* raised issues that had to be fought out in the hearts and minds of people as well as on the actual firing-lines."[4]

On the home front, the program involved recruiting and organizing seventy-five thousand speakers to make brief patriotic speeches, distributing seventy-five million pamphlets, publishing a newspaper, establishing a bureau of information that answered eighty-six thousand questions in ten months, and many other activities. Creel's committee also developed vigorous programs in numerous foreign countries including radio broadcasts, films, a news service, books for local libraries, and other initiatives.

In Mexico City a reading room was created as a center for the general dissemination of information. Located centrally, it was well equipped with tables, chairs, U.S. and Mexican newspapers and magazines, daily cable news, frequent lectures, films, and free toilets. It was surprisingly successful. "From the beginning the Reading Room was patronized to capacity day and evening. The visitors came from all ranks of citizens, artisans, laborers, shopkeepers, professional men, women, flocking there for enlightenment as to the issues, and progress of the war, and to exchange views of the situation," wrote Creel.[5] In the seven and a half months of its operation, it recorded 106,868 visitors. An equally popular school was added next door to teach English, bookkeeping, stenography, and French. Additional reading rooms, opened in six other Mexican cities, were also used heavily.[6] Creel celebrated all of these achievements in a book titled *How We Advertised America.*[7]

WORLD WAR II

Isolationism, distaste for propaganda, and politicians' negative reactions to Creel's vigorous efforts led to the prompt closure of the Committee on Public Information at the end of the war. But as the prospect of hostilities loomed again in the late 1930s, with growing concern at the prospect of German Nazi influence in Latin America, the U.S. government quietly helped revive Creel's ideas for foreign information policy.

In 1940, President Franklin D. Roosevelt appointed Nelson Rockefeller to a new position of coordinator of inter-American affairs (CIAA) in the Office of the Coordinator of Inter-American Affairs (OCIAA). In 1942, under the direction of Carl Milam, the executive secretary of the American Library Association, three libraries were established in Latin America starting with the Biblioteca Benjamin Franklin Library in Mexico City with five thousand volumes. (From the 1870s onward, American librarians and library organizations consistently and actively engaged in a wide variety of international activities and collaborations.)[8] Similar libraries in other countries followed, along with many reading rooms such as those pioneered by George Creel and his Committee on Public Information. Libraries were established in Havana, Port-au-Prince, São Paulo, Rio, Lima, and Caracas.

OFFICE OF WAR INFORMATION (OWI)

For areas outside Latin America, leadership was provided through two of President Roosevelt's appointees, "Wild Bill" Donovan and Archibald MacLeish. William Joseph Donovan (1885–1959) was an adventurous lawyer and soldier hired to create the Office for Strategic Services, the direct ancestor of the present Central Intelligence Agency.

Archibald MacLeish (1892–1982) was successful in many different roles: athlete, poet, lawyer, banker, and writer. In 1939, at President Roosevelt's insistence, he became the librarian of Congress. It was a controversial appointment, one that the leadership of the American Library Association fiercely opposed. However, a small group, the Progressive Librarians' Council, led by Philip Keeney, the university librarian at Montana State University in Missoula, vocally supported MacLeish's candidacy. MacLeish restructured, modernized, and gained increased funding for the library.[9] MacLeish combined this role with a deep involvement in a complicated series of initiatives and organizational changes for intelligence gathering and public information for which the Library of Congress provided space and practical support. When the United States entered World War II, MacLeish saw the Library of Congress as a war-related agency. He spoke of a "psychological front" in the war and urged "the strategy of truth."[10]

MacLeish also assisted with development of a new research and analysis branch of the Office of Strategic Services. He and others recruited a professional staff drawn from across the social sciences—including Philip Keeney—who were housed, in part, in the Library of Congress. MacLeish also served as director of the War Department's Office of Facts and Figures (OFF), which had been established to disseminate factual information on the defense effort and to facilitate widespread understanding of the status and progress of the war effort. MacLeish became assistant director of OFF's successor, the Office of War Information (OWI). These activities, heavily involved with propaganda, were well-suited to MacLeish's talents. In 1944 he left the Library of Congress for the State Department to be assistant secretary of state for public affairs, and he became engaged in the creation of UNESCO.

Chapter 5

OWI LIBRARIES AND INFORMATION CENTERS

In 1942 Roosevelt combined the Office of Facts and Figures with four other units to form an Office of War Information (OWI). Following the attack on Pearl Harbor in December 1941, the need for coordinated and properly disseminated wartime information from the government and the military to the public outweighed public distaste for propaganda. OWI was headed by journalist Elmer Davis with the mandate to take an active part in winning the war and in laying the foundations for a better postwar world.

In London, Richard Heindel developed a specialized library service dedicated to feeding useful information to political leaders, and OWI started other libraries elsewhere. In 1943 OWI established new information libraries in Melbourne, Sydney, Wellington, Cape Town, Johannesburg, Bombay, and, later, Cairo. The Department of State announced this move with the following explanation:

> The American Library in London and the five new libraries are designed to service writers, the press, radio, American missions, local government agencies, and cultural institutions and organizations. They are not lending-libraries for casual readers, nor are they in any sense propaganda centers or distributors of pamphlets. A small, highly selective library containing reference material produced in the United States provides information which can best reach the masses of people in an allied country through the media of the press, the radio, and educational institutions.[11]

A history of this effort provided a sharper assessment:

> The type of institution that Milam recommended, while not a radical departure from tradition, developed under the OWI into a different kind of overseas library. Whereas the American centers in Paris and Mexico City were modeled on the American public library and intended to build long-range cultural relations, the London library and other OWI collections were designed to provide the "mental sinews of total war," becoming principally reference libraries for the "purposive dissemination of information."[12]

Each library had about one thousand reference works and four thousand government documents on a wide range of topics, in addition to periodicals, pamphlets, maps, and other books. Other materials were collected for exhibits on, for example, the educational system in the United States. Each library had two well-qualified and experienced professional librarians with a mission to liaise with local institutions and to provide expert assistance. OWI successfully recruited able, engaged, effective librarians. Flora Belle Ludington, for example, the longtime director of Mount Holyoke College library and chair of the American Library Association's Board of International Relations, took leave to start the OWI library in Bombay. Eventually seventeen libraries worldwide were established.[13] In 1945, Heindel wrote:

> I think the O.W.I. work in the field adds up to the most significant development in American library history in the 1940's and probably 1950s. These outpost libraries were born of the war . . . but it seems clear that they are likely to be just as valuable in peace. . . . The O.W.I., by very practical and factual efforts, has carried the importance of libraries and books to the people and has raised them to a new and honorable position.[14]

Other major countries also used libraries and cultural centers abroad as part of their foreign cultural policy. The United Kingdom's British Council's library program was particularly effective. During the Cold War, U.S. libraries abroad repeatedly were denounced in the Soviet Union as sinister capitalist reactionary propaganda.[15]

The previous chapter used California as a case study of the development of library services within a region using the governmental structure of that region. This chapter examined the different situation of one country providing library service in other countries to advance its own foreign policy. The next chapters are concerned with the more complex situation during the Allied occupation of Japan, 1945–1952, where two culturally and politically different governments were concerned with the development of library policy for the same country and the use of OWI-style libraries as a means of exerting cultural pressure.

NOTES

1. Quoted in Sidney H. Ditzion, *Arsenals of a Democratic Culture: A Social History of the American Public Library Movement in New England and the Middle States from 1850 to 1900* (Chicago: American Library Association, 1947), vi.

2. John W. Gaddis, *Public Information in Japan under American Occupation: A Study of Democratization Efforts through Agencies of Public Expression* (Geneva: Imprimeries Populaires, 1950), 56.

3. There is an extensive literature on U.S. cultural foreign policy. General works include American Assembly, *Cultural Affairs and Foreign Relations* (Englewood Cliffs, NJ: Prentice-Hall, 1963); Nicholas Cull, *The Cold War and the U.S. Information Agency: American Propaganda and Public Diplomacy, 1945–1989* (Cambridge: Cambridge University Press, 2008); Robert E. Elder, *The Information Machine: The United States Information Agency and American Foreign Policy* (Syracuse, NY: Syracuse University Press, 1968); J. Manuel Espinosa, *Inter-American Beginnings of U.S. Cultural Diplomacy: 1936–1948* (Washington, DC: Government Printing Office, 1976); Fred J. Harsaghy, "The Administration of American Cultural Projects Abroad" (PhD diss., New York University, 1985); Justin Hart, *Empire of Ideas: The Origins of Public Diplomacy and the Transformation of U.S. Foreign Policy* (Oxford: Oxford University Press, 2013); John W. Henderson, *The United States Information Agency* (New York: Praeger, 1969); Ruth E. McMurry and Muna Lee, *The Cultural Approach: Another Way in International Relations* (Chapel Hill: University of North Carolina Press, 1947); Frank A. Ninkovich, *The Diplomacy of Ideas: U.S. Foreign Policy and Cultural Relations, 1938–1950* (New York: Cambridge University Press, 1981); Douglas Schneider, "America's

Answer to Communist Propaganda Abroad," *Department of State Bulletin*, 19 (December 19, 1948): 772–76; Charles A. Thomson and Walter H. C. Laves, *Cultural Relations and U. S. Foreign Policy* (Bloomington: Indiana University Press, 1963). For the use of libraries and information services in cultural diplomacy, see Beverly J. Brewster, *American Overseas Library Technical Assistance, 1940–1970* (Metuchen, NJ: Scarecrow Press, 1976); Joan Collet, "American Libraries Abroad: United States Information Agency Activities," *Library Trends* 20, no. 3 (January 1972): 538–47; Donald C. Hausrath, "United States International Communication Agency," 70–112, in *Encyclopedia of Library and Information Science*, vol. 32 (1981); Richard H. Heindel, "U.S. Libraries Overseas," *Survey Graphic*, 35 (May 1946): 162–65; Henry James, "The Role of the Information Library in the United States International Information Program," *Library Quarterly* 23, no. 2 (April 1953): 75–114; Gary E. Kraske, *Missionaries of the Book: The American Library Profession and the Origins of United States Cultural Diplomacy* (Westport, CT: Greenwood, 1985); Paxton Price, ed., *International Book and Library Activities: The History of a U.S. Foreign Policy* (Metuchen, NJ: Scarecrow Press, 1982); Oren Stephens, *Facts to a Candid World: America's Overseas Information Program* (Stanford, CA: Stanford University Press, 1955); and Charles A. H. Thomson, *Overseas Information Service of the United States Government* (Washington, DC: Brookings Institution, 1948). For U.S. cultural foreign policy with Japan, see Takeshi Matsuda, *Soft Power and Its Perils: U.S. Cultural Policy in Early Postwar Japan and Permanent Dependency* (Washington, DC: Woodrow Wilson Center Press, 2007).

4. George Creel, *How We Advertised America* (New York: Harper, 1920), 3, https://catalog.hathitrust.org/Record/000005455.

5. Creel, *How We Advertised America*, 314.

6. United States. Committee on Public Information. *Complete Report of the Chairman of the Committee on Public Information: 1917, 1918, 1919* (Washington, DC: Government Printing Office, 1920), 161–62, https://catalog.hathitrust.org/Record/009600453.

7. Creel, *How We Advertised America*.

8. For a concise history, see Flora Belle Ludington, "The American Contribution to Foreign Library Establishment and Rehabilitation," *Library Quarterly* 24, no. 2 (April 1954): 192–204.

9. For MacLeish at the Library of Congress, see Scott Donaldson, *Archibald MacLeish: An American Life* (Boston: Houghton Mifflin, 1992); Frederick J. Stielow, "Librarian Warriors and Rapprochement: Carl Milam, Archibald MacLeish and World War II," *Libraries and Culture* 25, no. 4 (Fall 1990): 513–33; and Frederick J. Stielow, "MacLeish, Archibald (1892–1982)," 59–63, in *Dictionary of American Library Biography: Supplement*, edited by Wayne A. Wiegand (Englewood, CO: Libraries Unlimited, 1990).

10. Archibald MacLeish, "The Strategy of Truth," 19–31, in *A Time to Act: Selected Addresses*, edited by Archibald MacLeish (Boston: Houghton Mifflin, 1943).

11. "United States Information Libraries Abroad," *Department of State Bulletin* 9, no. 223 (October 2, 1943): 228–29, http://catalog.hathitrust.org/Record/000598610.

12. Kraske, *Missionaries of the Book*, 140.

13. Ruth M. Gurin, and H. M. Baumgartner, "U.S. Information Libraries Prove Their Worth," *Library Journal* 71, no. 3 (February 1, 1946): 137–41; Cedric Larson, "Books across the Sea: Libraries of the OWI," *Wilson Library Bulletin* 25, no. 2 (February 1951): 433–36; Ludington, "American Contribution"; Pamela Spence Richards, "Information for the Allies: Office of War Information Libraries in Australia, New Zealand, and South Africa," *Library Quarterly* 52, no. 4 (October 1982): 325–47; and Allan M. Winkler, *The Politics of Propaganda: The Office of War Information, 1942–1945* (New Haven, CT: Yale University Press, 1978).

14. Quoted in Richards, "Information for the Allies," 330.

15. The Soviet library science journal *Bibliothekar* has several articles denouncing U.S. use of libraries for cultural foreign policy in the late 1940s and 1950s.

Chapter Six

Libraries in Japan and the Allied Occupation

At present, though Japan possesses a large string of libraries, it cannot be said that these institutions are adequate and fully equipped from the scientific standpoint. Indeed, the time has come for exercising co-ordinated control over all the libraries in the country for the larger benefit of national enlightenment.
—Takebayashi Kumahiko, April 1945 [1]

LIBRARIES IN JAPAN

Japan has a long tradition of scholarship and, after the Meiji Restoration of 1868, a very high literacy rate; a well-developed publishing industry; plentiful, popular bookstores; and a tradition of buying and selling used books. It also has a long tradition of private collections of religious and scholarly materials that scholars would be allowed to use. Foreign library developments, especially in the United States, were well known to at least a few librarians, but libraries seem to have been of relatively little interest to the government. Interest in public libraries, as well as university and specialized libraries, increased significantly after 1900 following a Library Law in 1899. Nevertheless, the idea of libraries as service agencies and librarianship as a service profession made little progress during the Meiji period (1868–1912) and were not seen as important for the authoritarian school system influenced by French and German educational practices.[2] As one Japanese scholar puts it,

> The highly nationalistic system of education which came into being [in 1866] remained in effect for the next sixty years without substantial changes. . . . All national wealth, interest and strength were directed toward competition with

the Western powers and eventually war with China and Russia. Culture then was recognized only in an auxiliary, or appendant role. Education was a means to achieve that national policy. When education becomes a means to implement national policies, and thus discourages independent thinking and research, the development of modern libraries will be curtailed.[3]

Early in 1945 a positive Japanese account of the modern library movement in Japan by Takebayashi Kumahiko noted the founding of various libraries and Japanese resilience in avoiding Western ideas incompatible with Japanese spirit. He nevertheless concluded:

> At present, though Japan possesses a large string of libraries, it cannot be said that these institutions are adequate and fully equipped from the scientific standpoint. Indeed, the time has come for exercising co-ordinated control over all the libraries in the country for the larger benefit of national enlightenment.[4]

As of 1945, the one national library was the Imperial Library in Ueno Park, which had about five hundred thousand volumes in Japanese and Chinese and about one hundred thousand volumes of foreign publications.

University library collections grew rapidly in the early twentieth century, but in 1950 the Ministry of Education commented harshly on the state of university main library services and on the tradition of having, as in German universities, many small, separate departmental, "attached" libraries controlled by autocratic professors.

> Most of the old-system universities had complete libraries, each of which had books amounting to more than 500,000 volumes. As has already been pointed out by the Human Culture Advisory Commission, these libraries were mostly negative in their activities, too independent from each other, whose books were mainly fragmentary collections of documents, too narrow in their specific fields of interest, whose finances were apt to be neglected, whose improvements had been fantastically partial, and whose personnel had to be fundamentally re-educated so that they might have knowledge and experience necessary for each of the specific fields of librarian duty, along with the education of the specialists in this field. . . . As to the attached libraries, many of them have been lost during the war times most of their books as well as their facilities, without any means left for supplementing new books, periodicals and especially printed materials from overseas, the result being that they are deplorable [*sic*] deficient for use. . . . with so many dispersed branch libraries, the organic functions of all of which have been naturally hampered beyond description.[5]

The library law of 1899 authorized local governments to establish public libraries at their own expense. The Ministry of Education issued a handbook on librarianship in 1900 and sponsored a summer school in 1908. By 1927 Japan had some 4,300 libraries. In 1949, just before the new Library Law of 1950, Japan had 1,549 public libraries, some privately operated, in the forty-six prefectures with total holdings of 8,824,528 books for an average size of around 5,700. However, the great majority of the libraries would have been much smaller because the totals include the larger prefectural libraries. They operated independently and had very low daily attendance.[6]

They did not resemble contemporary public library service in the United States or in Great Britain. They were stores of books and not designed for browsing. Because librarians could be personally liable for missing books, readers normally did not have access to the shelves ("open access"). Books not kept in rooms inaccessible to readers (closed access) commonly were on "semi-open" shelving with wire grills covering the front of the shelves so that readers could see, but not touch, what was on the shelves. One had to ask library staff to obtain a book.

Many public libraries were operated privately, not by local governments. Small fees commonly were charged for membership and/or for borrowing. In general, they were collections rather than library services. In the first half of the twentieth century, neither the education system nor the increasingly authoritarian political regime was conducive to the free exploration and expression of ideas that are central to Anglophone public library traditions. The concept of reference service was lacking.[7] Nevertheless, to activists in France struggling without success to promote public libraries, the Japanese library scene could be pointed to for comparison. "Burdened by the prodigious effort of its triumph," wrote Eugène Morel after the Russo-Japanese war of 1904–1905, "Japan has not yet forgotten its material of triumph. It buys cannons and it buys books."[8]

School libraries were associated with literacy—as a resource for learning to read, a different orientation from our present emphasis on libraries as a place for discovery, as a resource for finding out. They existed outside the curriculum. In practice they were collections of unused books in a locked case. A secondary school with more than five hundred books and pamphlets for the use of pupils in addition to its textbooks was rare. The concept of a school library for use by all pupils scarcely existed, and secondary schools had no full-time, paid professional school librarians.[9]

The development of special libraries outside educational contexts is not well documented. Many small collections must have played an important role, given the heavy use of imported and translated technical books. The outstanding exception was the documentation center supporting the research department in Tokyo of the South Manchuria Railway (known as Mantetsu) with an exceptionally rich collection of some two hundred thousand volumes. This was far more than a railway company library. This research center was concerned with planning the development of the Japanese empire.[10]

Libraries used diverse local classification schemes, including many different adaptions of the Dewey Decimal Classification. Even the leading library classification, the Nippon Decimal Classification, was used by only a few libraries.

About half of all library buildings had been destroyed in the war, and some surviving library buildings had been taken over for other purposes. About half of all collections were lost. Librarianship was not regarded as a profession, and librarians were poorly paid.

TRAINING OF LIBRARIANS

There had been little training for library work before 1945, and what little there was had focused on technical procedures.[11] A two-week course initially offered by the Japan Library Association in 1903 was provided repeatedly. A course in librarianship at the University of Tokyo (then Tokyo Imperial University) was offered from 1918 to 1922 by Wada Mankichi, who had been trained at Harvard University library. After that, the only training program for librarians was a one-year program offered by the Library Training Institute, which started in 1922 and later moved into the national library in Ueno Park. In 1941 it was shortened to nine months, then suspended. The requirement for admission had been low—graduation from middle school—which could be waived for applicants with library experience. The curriculum focused on library methods of acquisition, cataloging and classification, book arts, and some historical and educational topics, with practice work during the last two months. Maximum enrollment was thirty, and the program lapsed during the war. The League of Young Librarians (Seinen Toshokan'in Remei), led by Mamiya Fujio, had taken the initiative to provide useful manuals on acquisitions, classification, and cataloging.

A very few Japanese librarians had studied in library education programs abroad. A few others had work experience in the United States, as Wada had. One who appears repeatedly in the following pages, Naomi Fukuda, had both. She went to the United States, where she obtained a second BA in history and a master of library science degree from the University of Michigan, then worked for several months at the Library of Congress.[12] Japanese librarians, or at least the leaders, were aware of overseas developments in the United States and elsewhere.

THE OCCUPATION

During the war, the United States made elaborate preparations for the redirection of Japanese society after the war. It included a strongly idealistic, liberal ideology, a continuation of Roosevelt's New Deal. Japan had to be reoriented away from its militaristic, antidemocratic ways into a Western liberal democracy. Similar aspirations within Japan largely had been suppressed from the early 1920s by successive militaristic, totalitarian governments. If the existing social and political order of Japan remained intact, Japan would have no prospect of democracy. The allied powers' Potsdam Declaration of July 26, 1945, defining terms for Japanese surrender called not only for surrender but also political change: "The Japanese Government shall remove all obstacles to the revival and strengthening of democratic tendencies among the Japanese people."

If Japan was to be disarmed, demilitarized, and set on the road to a peaceful democratic state, control over the emperor and a free hand to change the political, social, and economic conditions of Japan were needed. The Allied agenda was very clearly and firmly stated in the instructions President Truman sent to General MacArthur in early September 1945, titled *U.S. Initial Surrender Policy for Japan*.[13] Senior officials were equally explicit. The director of the State Department's Office of Far Eastern Affairs, John Carter Vincent, stated in a radio broadcast:

> Our immediate goal is to demobilize the Japanese armed forces and demilitarize Japan. Our long-range objective is to *democratize* Japan—to encourage democratic self-government. . . . The occupation will continue until demobilization and demilitarization are completed. And it will continue until there is assurance that Japan is well along the path of liberal reform.

The Allied forces already had made very substantial relevant preparation for the ideological role of democratizing, including psychological warfare, orientation, military government, and, specifically, using libraries as a vehicle for cultural diplomacy. A well-known example of their psychological warfare was the dropping of many millions of carefully designed leaflets by Allied aerial forces onto areas still occupied by Japanese forces. These were designed to undermine the morale of Japanese soldiers and to encourage them to surrender. Less well known is the intensive orientation of Allied troops. Orientation was designed to ensure that all members of the armed services had the right ideas about the purpose and proper conduct of the war effort. In the Pacific theater, every single regiment had a full-time information and education officer, and having a second full-time officer was authorized. Unless currently engaged in active combat, all ranks were required to undertake a full hour of indoctrination every week.

An information and education section in the central command supplied the information officers with a steady supply of talking points and resource material through *Maptalk*, a magazine distributed only to these officers. As the date of the expected invasion approached, a series of large supplementary pamphlets were issued on the geopolitics of the Pacific theater, Japan's recent political and military history, cultural attitudes of the Japanese, and what to expect when in Japan. Titles of the *Maptalk* supplements included *Objec-*

tive Japan; This Is the Land That Breeds Him; Japan Plots to Conquer: This Is Why He Fights; and *National Hari-kiri*, on Japan's modern history since the invasion of Manchuria; also *Cherry Blossoms and Samurai Swords*, which, it explains, "is concerned with the sort of people that history has produced"; *Greater East Asia: The Tangled Web*, on the geography of combat zones and Japanese-controlled areas; and *How Strong Is Japan? Estimated Strength & Resources*.[14]

MILITARY GOVERNMENT

Both the U.S. Army and Navy invested heavily in advanced training. By 1943 technical training programs for military personnel had been established at three hundred colleges with a capacity of two hundred thousand students in a wide range of specialties.

When the Allied forces invaded Italy from North Africa and fought their way north, local government largely collapsed, requiring the invading Allied army to improvise civil government. The same experience occurred in the invasion of Germany and the numerous Pacific islands of the Japanese empire. The U.S. Army developed a new military specialty in the civil administration of occupied areas, known as "civil affairs" or as "military government." The Army's provost marshal general established training programs.

The Allied occupation of Japan differed from the occupation of Germany in important ways. Germany was divided into four zones administered by Britain, France, Russia, and the United States, respectively. Germany was a European country controlled by three other European countries and by the United States with its heavily European cultural heritage and its large German-American population. Knowledge of German and about Germany was common in the occupying countries. In contrast, the occupation of Japan, while officially an Allied effort, was, in practice, a U.S. effort. Unlike the underlying cultural similarities of Germany and its occupiers, Japan's culture, history, and language were different and alien. As of 1945, the United States had very few experts on Japanese culture and society, and because they were considered to be conservative and unreliable, they were largely disregarded in the State Department and in the general headquarters of Supreme Commander for Allied Powers (SCAP).

For military government in Japan, army and navy officers aged thirty-five or older who already had administrative experience of some kind completed an initial orientation in military government at the School of Military Government at the University of Virginia in Charlottesville. Each then completed an intensive six-month preparation at one of six programs at Chicago, Harvard, Michigan, Northwestern, Stanford, or Yale Universities. The curriculum covered spoken Japanese, Japanese society and culture, and civil administration. The program included planning exercises specific to possible problems in Japan. Highly expert instructors were used, supplemented by interned Japanese nationals as teaching assistants.[15] About twenty-five hundred officers completed this training and were sent to the Civil Affairs Holding and Staging Area (CASA) in Monterey, California, ready for the invasion of Japan being planned for November 1945.

With the unexpected Japanese surrender in August and the immediate appointment of General MacArthur as supreme commander for the Allied powers (SCAP) on August 15, 1945, three hundred military government specialists prepared for work in Japan were rushed to Manila. As a practical necessity, SCAP was obliged to govern through the intact existing Japanese governmental apparatus rather than engage in direct military government. This made the powerful Japanese civilian bureaucracy, which remained largely untouched, even more powerful.[16] MacArthur was able on arrival in Tokyo to act very rapidly on a wide range of changes only because of the extensive planning.[17] Half of the officers prepared for military government in Japan were reassigned to Korea. The remainder formed much of the initial leadership of the SCAP general headquarters. Administratively, MacArthur controlled two different organizations, a military command and a civil command. They both reported to him but were kept quite separate.

A deeply rooted cultural difference that largely undermined efforts at educational reform was the deeply held American association of democracy with individualism and with the decentralization of government. Another was the centralization of power in Japan, as in France, and the conscious adoption of the strongly hierarchical model of bureaucracy that Max Weber had made famous. An authoritarian, hierarchical bureaucracy does not accommodate independent-minded professionals well. In the event, the liberal ideals in wartime Washington were hindered by the practical reality of a deeply different culture, practical difficulties, SCAP Commander General Douglas MacArthur's emphasis on military issues, and then the displacement of idealistic goals by the Cold War, an obsession with the threat of Communism, and hostilities in neighboring Korea.

JAPANESE LIBRARIANS

Libraries in Japan in 1945 did not resemble libraries in the United States or Britain, nor did the training of librarians or their status. Quite apart from the wartime destruction, the high costs of the militaristic period and a different, more authoritarian approach to education at all levels inhibited the development of libraries along U.S. lines. But that does not mean that librarians did not have the same or similar aspirations. In 1926 Matsumoto Kiichi, director of the Imperial Library, addressing the American Library Association annual meeting on library developments in Japan, said:

> I have candidly to say that the new libraries were founded after the pattern of American libraries in their constitution and contents, in their equipment and methods, that is to say, in most things.[18]

Takebayashi Kumahiko, writing during the war about Japan's modern library movement, was more guarded. Western ideas were adopted when compatible with Japanese character and tradition, he wrote, noting Japanese resilience in avoiding Western ideas incompatible with Japanese spirit.[19]

The American librarians chronicled in this book doubtless saw themselves as bringing something valuable from U.S. librarianship to Japan. They were impressed by the receptiveness and initiative of librarians in Japan and tended to see weaknesses in Japanese library service as a product of political, social, and economic forces and traditions far beyond librarians' control.

Takeuchi Satoru, a dedicated Japanese librarian and library educator, received a master of library science degree from Florida State University and his PhD from Pittsburgh University in 1979. His very detailed doctoral dissertation on education for librarianship in Japan before and after 1945 draws almost exclusively on Japanese sources. He makes clear that, as of 1946, Japanese librarians were familiar with the development of libraries in the United States and that they effectively used occupation library advisers to achieve their own plans, even though they were largely thwarted by the conservatism and austerity of Japanese government, not least in the Library Law of 1950 that substituted shadow for substance.[20]

Our previous chapter outlined the U.S. experience deploying small, attractive libraries in foreign countries as a vehicle for cultural and political influence. That prior experience enabled the occupying forces to start providing that kind of library in Japan with remarkable speed, as will be described in the next chapter.

NOTES

1. I follow the surname before forename style for Japanese names except when the Western forename before surname is well established; for example, Naomi Fukuda.

2. For a fuller account in English, see Theodore F. Welch, *Libraries and Librarianship in Japan* (Westport, CT: Greenwood, 1997); and his earlier *Toshokan: Libraries in Japanese Society* (London: Bingley, 1976); also, Suzuki Yukihisa, "American Influence on the Development of Library Services in Japan 1860–1948" (PhD diss., University of Michigan, 1956); Louise W. Tung, "Library Development in Japan," *Library Quarterly* 26, no. 2 (April 1956): 79–104, and *Library Quarterly* 26, no. 3 (July 1956): 196–223. For a concise summary as of 1926, see Miyogo Ohsa, "On the Libraries in Japan," *ALA Bulletin* 20, no. 10 (October 1926): 244–51. Satoru Takeuchi, "Education for Librarianship in Japan: A Comparative Study of the Pre-1945 and Post-1945 Periods" (PhD diss., University of Pittsburgh, 1979) is very useful beyond education because of its detail, and it is based almost entirely on Japanese sources. A

shorter version is his "Japan, Education for Library and Information Science," 239–71, in *Encyclopedia of Library and Information Science*, vol. 36 (New York: Marcel Dekker, 1983). For this and following chapters, see especially Kon Madoko and Masaya Takayama, eds., *Gendai Nihon no toshokan kōsō: sengo kaikaku to sono tenkai* [The Library Conception in Modern Japan: The Postwar Reformation and Its Development] (Tokyo: Bensei Shuppan, 2013), which mentions many U.S. librarians, especially 102–50.

3. Suzuki, "American Influence,"135.

4. Takebayashi Kumahiko, "Modern Japan and Library Movement," *Contemporary Japan*, 14 (April–December 1945): 233. See also Sharon Domier, "From Reading Guidance to Thought Control: Wartime Japanese Libraries," *Library Trends* 55, no. 3 (Winter 2007): 551–69.

5. Japan, Ministry of Education, *Progress of Education Reform in Japan* (Tokyo: Ministry of Education, 1950), 53–54.

6. Japan, *Progress of Education*, table 21, 152. The data, which does not include the average daily attendance of prefectural central libraries, implies for the remainder an average daily attendance of six.

7. Sano Tomosaburo, "The Public Library in Japan," *Public Libraries* 14, no. 6 (June 1909): 214; Ronald S. Anderson, *Japan: Three Epochs of Modern Education* (Washington, DC: U.S. Department of Health, Education, and Welfare, Office of Education, 1959); Domier, "From Reading Guidance to Thought Control."

8. Eugène Morel, *Bibliothèques, essai sur le développement des bibliothèques publiques et de la librairie dans les deux mondes*, vol. 1 (Paris: Mercure de France, 1908–1909), 389: "Obéré par l'effort prodigieux de son triomphe, le Japon n'a pourtant pas oublié son material de triomphe, il achète des canons et il achète des livres," http://catalog.hathitrust.org/Record/001164300.

9. Supreme Commander for the Allied Powers, Civil Information and Education Section, Education Division, *Education in the New Japan*, vol. 1 (Tokyo: General Headquarters, Supreme Commander for the Allied Powers, Civil Information and Education Section, Education Division, 1948), 78–79.

10. Hara Kakuten, *Gendai Ajia kenkyū seiritsu shiron: Mantetsu Chōsabu, Tōa Kenkyūjo, IPR no kenkyū* (Tokyo: Keiso Shobo, 1984), 426–74; and Takayama Masaya, *Rekishi ni miru Nihon no toshokan: chiteki seika no juyō to denshō* (Tokyo: Keiso Shobo), 59–76.

11. Sawamoto Takahisa, "Training and Education Programs for Librarians in Japan," 65–72, in *Library Education in Developing Countries*, edited by George S. Bonn (Honolulu: East-West Center Press, 1966); also, Takeuchi, *Education*; Takeuchi, *Japan*; Suzuki, "American Influence"; Ohsa, "On the Libraries"; and *Toshokan jōhōgaku kyōiku no sengoshi: shiryō ga kataru senmonshoku yōsei seido no tenkai*, edited by Akira Nemoto (Kyoto: Mineruva Shobō, 2015), 2–3.

12. For Naomi Fukuda, see Koide Izumi, "Catalyst for the Professionalization of Librarianship in Postwar Japan: Naomi Fukuda and the United States Field Seminar of 1959," *Asian Cultural Studies*, 39 (March 2013): 65–78; and Kon Madoko, [Eulogy of Fukuda], *International House of Japan Bulletin* 27, no. 2 (2007): 46–48.

13. "U.S. Initial Surrender Policy for Japan," *Department of State Bulletin* 13, no. 326 (September 23, 1945): 423–27, https://catalog.hathitrust.org/Record/000598610; J. C. Vincent, J. H. Hilldring, and R. L. Dennison, "Our Occupation Policy for Japan," *Department of State Bulletin* 13, no. 328 (October 7, 1945): 538–45, https://catalog.hathitrust.org/Record/000598610. The literature on the Allied occupation is very large. For English-language materials, *The Allied Occupation of Japan, 1945–1952: An Annotated Bibliography of Western-Language Materials*, edited by Robert E. Ward and Frank J. Shulman (Chicago: American Library Association, 1974).

14. *Maptalk* (n.p.: United States Army, Forces, Far East, Information and Education Section, 1–5 (1944–1946) and *Supplements* 1–5 (1945).

15. For what the instructors knew or believed, see a thorough, well-written summary by nine of them published after the end of the war in *Japan's Prospect*, edited by Douglas G. Haring (Cambridge, MA: Harvard University Press, 1946).

16. John W. Dower, *Embracing Defeat: Japan in the Wake of World War II* (New York: Norton, 1999), 223.

17. Merle Fainsod, "Military Government and the Occupation of Japan," 287–304, in *Japan's Prospect*, edited by Douglas G. Haring (Cambridge, MA: Harvard University Press, 1946); also, Hajo Holborn, *American Military Government: Its Organization and Policies* (Washington, DC: Infantry Journal Press, 1947), 87–99; Malcolm M. Willey, "The College Training Programs of the Armed Services," *Annals of the American Academy of Political and Social Science*, 231 (January 1944): 14–28; Justin Williams, "From Charlottesville to Tokyo: Military Government Training and Democratic Reforms in Occupied Japan," *Pacific Historical Review*, 51 (1982): 407–22.

18. Matsumoto Kiichi, "Libraries and Library Work in Japan," *ALA Bulletin* 20, no. 10 (October 1926): 243.

19. Takebayashi, "Modern Japan."

20. Takeuchi, "Education for Librarianship"; Takeuchi, "Japan."

Chapter Seven

CIE Information Centers

A full and fair picture of American life and of the aims and policies of the United States Government. —President Harry S. Truman, October 21, 1945 [1]

The U.S. Office of War Information (OWI) was engaged with Japan before the end of the war. Inside Japan the media were tightly controlled by the government, but official propaganda was ineffective.[2] One reason was incompetence. Another was a lack of respect for truthful facts. An experienced OWI staff member, John F. Sullivan, wrote of Japanese ministries' pre-surrender propaganda efforts:

> Accustomed to thinking in terms of centralized propaganda, distortions of facts, and suppression of news, the [Japanese] government was not prepared to adopt as one of its legitimate functions the dissemination of information which would assist the people to think, to question, and to form opinions. . . . The art or science of public relations was completely unknown. . . . There were occasional press releases, reports and 'white papers,' stodgily written and generally over the heads of the masses. There was a total absence of coordination.[3]

The stronger the social control and the stronger the government's power, the less the likely concern for what the general population knows. But effective propaganda requires some elements of factual basis to be credible. Near the end of the war, military defeats were no longer claimed as victories, but the dire military and economic situation was not revealed. Awareness of the harsh facts was advanced by the increasing effectiveness of OWI, whose pamphlets dropped from airplanes were dramatic and factual.[4]

SCAP GHQ CIVIL INFORMATION AND EDUCATION SECTION

In this situation and given the mission to promote a democratic culture in Japan, public information and education had to be serious concerns for the Allied occupation. Japan had surrendered in mid-August 1945, and the Instrument of Surrender was signed on September 2. Field Marshal Douglas MacArthur became Supreme Commander for Allied Powers (SCAP) and established his general headquarters (GHQ) in Tokyo.[5] His mandate, the basic initial post-surrender directive of November 1, 1945, included instructions concerning propaganda, censorship, freedom of opinion, speech, press, and assembly.[6]

Within the SCAP general headquarters, a Civil Information and Education section (CIE) was created on September 22 "to advise the Supreme Commander on policies relating to public information, education, religion and other sociological problems of Japan." The specific charges included:

> 3.a. Make recommendations to: (1) Effect the accomplishments of the information and educational objectives of the Allied Powers. (2) Expedite the establishment of freedom of religious worship, freedom of opinion, speech, press and assembly by dissemination of democratic ideals and principles through all media of public information. . . . b. Make recommendations on information problems, through all media, reaching the Japanese public.[7]

This mandate required reforms to remove restrictive controls, including abolition of the Cabinet Board of Information, but the primary means was an emphasis on best practices for a democratic society. A press code and a radio code were issued within the first month of the occupation stipulating factual, truthful, and unbiased reporting, and a degree of censorship was used to monitor compliance with the codes.

CIE was staffed by a range of specialists, each charged to address issues within his sphere. A CIE specialist was expected to analyze actual or potential problems, consult within SCAP GHQ, with counterparts in the Japanese government, and with any other interested parties, and, when appropriate, make recommendations that would be considered within the SCAP GHQ hierarchy and, if appropriate, transmitted to the Japanese government for action. Libraries were mentioned only in the final sentence of the CIE directive.

> g. Make recommendations to the Supreme Commander on matters relating to the protection, preservation, salvage or other disposition of works of arts and antiquity, cultural treasures, religious articles, libraries, museums, archival repositories, religious buildings and historical monuments.[8]

Nevertheless, the first OWI-style library in Japan was opened with remarkable speed. CIE opened its first library for the Japanese public in Tokyo on November 15. John W. Gaddis, chief of the policy and programs branch of CIE's information division, described CIE's libraries as being

> created to further democratization through modern knowledge, especially a knowledge of recent literary, technical and political works of a kind not available to the Japanese during the hysterical 1930's and '40s and never available in quantity even in the relatively liberal decade up to 1930.[9]

Colonel Kenneth R. Dyke was appointed chief of the CIE, which had two divisions: civil information and education. The first head of the civil information division was Bradford Smith, who had been chief of OWI's Central Pacific operations in Manila and had joined the State Department when it absorbed OWI in late August 1945. Smith brought with him a team of OWI propaganda experts that included his successor as head of CIE's information division, Don Brown. Libraries were part of the information division and thus the responsibility of Bradford Smith and later Don Brown.

The first library was opened even before its collection was ready. For a while only a collection of armed services editions was available. Some 122 million copies of more than thirteen hundred different titles had been edited and printed inexpensively for distribution to the U.S. armed services by an American nonprofit organization, the Council on Books in Wartime. The intention was to provide entertainment to soldiers serving overseas, while also educating them about political, historical, and military issues. The council's slogan was "Books are weapons in the war of ideas." Some seventy publishers and a dozen printing houses collaborated to deliver mass-produced paperbacks selected by a panel of literary experts from among classics, best sellers, humor, and poetry, and made available only to servicemen and women serving outside the United States. Spare capacity in presses printing comic books was used to print two works at a time, one above the other, which were then cut into two landscape format paperbacks.[10]

Two factors made it possible to open this first library so rapidly. One was the extensive experience with the libraries and information centers that OWI developed in Latin America and elsewhere. The other was the detailed planning for the deployment of libraries in Japan well before the surrender. One person engaged in that planning was a former journalist, Don Brown.

DON BROWN

Donald Beckworth Brown (1905–1980) graduated from the University of Pittsburgh with a BA in journalism. After graduate study, he decided to work as a journalist in Britain. But first, in 1930, he went on vacation in China,

Figure 7.1. Don Brown.

where he met Wilfred Fleischer who recruited him to work at the *Japan Advertizer*, an English-language newspaper in Tokyo founded in 1908 by his father, Benjamin W. Fleischer. Following a nervous breakdown, the senior Fleisher had been advised by his doctor to travel. So, leaving his family in Paris, Benjamin Fleischer set off. Reaching Japan, he was charmed by Yokohama and its colony of European and North American expatriates. The colony had rival newsletters, and Fleischer helped in the production of one them. The outcome was that he acquired control of the newsletter, moved its production to Tokyo, used the most modern production techniques available, and made it the most-respected English-language newspaper in the Far East despite its production facility being twice destroyed by fire and by earthquake. Fleischer specialized in hiring young American journalism school graduates. Benjamin's son Wilfred became editor. In time, as the Japanese government became more militaristic and more authoritarian, newspapers with independent editorial policies were less and less acceptable. They and their employees were increasingly intimidated and harassed. In October 1940 Benjamin Fleischer was forced to sell the *Japan Advertizer* at a low price to the *Japan Times*, a newspaper loyal to the government.[11]

Don Brown was among the last of the American journalists to leave Japan before the outbreak of war. During the war he worked on media for psychological warfare in the Pacific theater, including leaflets dropped on islands occupied by Japanese soldiers. With the occupation of Japan, Don Brown joined the information division of the civil information and education section of the SCAP GHQ and soon became its head.[12]

PAUL BURNETTE

Within the information division of CIE was a library branch intended to promote access to modern knowledge, especially recent literary, technical, and political works. The library branch created its own facilities in the tradition of OWI libraries. The first CIE library in Japan was called a library, but later, as more such libraries were created, they were called information centers.

The first CIE library in Japan was planned and directed by Paul Jean Burnette (1908–1992), who, like Don Brown, will appear repeatedly in the pages that follow. Burnette obtained his graduate library degree at the University of Illinois, Urbana-Champaign, and then worked as a librarian at Montana State College in Bozeman when Philip Keeney was university librarian at the nearby Missoula campus. In his time, the standard qualification for librarians was a one-year postbaccalaureate certificate in librarianship (later redesignated bachelor of library science), but a few of the more ambitious librarians undertook additional work toward an MA in library science. In 1941 Burnette began additional study at the school of librarianship at the University of California, Berkeley, where he would have been influenced by Sydney Mitchell, its founding director, who set the school's tone. Mitchell was a wise, practical man with charm and unusual people skills.

In 1942 Burnette joined the Army Air Force and prepared for civil administration in Japan at the civil affairs training school, Far Eastern program (Japan), at the University of Michigan. On completion he was sent to the civil affairs holding and staging area (CASA) in Monterey, California, a small historic town a hundred miles south of San Francisco, to await transport to Japan.[13]

Chapter 7
CIE INFORMATION CENTERS

Although the collection at the first library in Tokyo initially had been a meager set of armed services editions, a more mature collection soon was assembled. A CIE information center would have about six thousand volumes of American books and periodicals. It was much more than a passive collection of books.[14] The centers were part of the occupation's civil information and education program and included active outreach. Service was free, and American occupation personnel were not admitted. The SCAP official history reported proudly on the first information center:

> Open to the general public, it particularly attracted students, teachers, editors and officials seeking information about American life or improvement of their knowledge of English. The value of the library to the Japanese public was so evident that SCAP in August 1947, stating that the Tokyo library attracted more readers daily than the largest Japanese public library, directed the Government to arrange facilities for similar libraries in Kyoto and Nagoya. In December 14 more libraries, to be established at government expense, were ordered for Fukuoka, Sendai, Sapporo, Takamatsu, Hiroshima, Osaka, Yokohama, Kobe, Niigata, Kanazawa, Kumamoto, Hakodate, Shizuoka and Nagasaki. All the libraries were to be staffed by Japanese who would be subordinate to the librarians assigned by SCAP. The Tokyo Library, at the same time, was placed on the same status as the others, to be maintained by the Japanese themselves. The last of the 17 libraries was opened 30 October 1948.[15]

It was not only the presentation of an attractive, up-to-date collection that caused interest, but a public library collection of books and magazines readily accessible on open shelves.

By the end of the occupation in April 1952, twenty-three were in highly visible operation. The information center in Osaka, for example, was located in a quiet financial district, so to attract attention an exhibit about the U.S. press was arranged in a large, popular department store with issues of a hundred newspapers and colorful magazines, and tables and chairs for reading. In addition to educational posters, it included an exhibit about the local information center, and films about U.S. schools and about the Library of Congress were screened twice a day. The exhibit was publicized with radio announcements, streetcar advertisements, a banner over the entrance to the store, public announcements within the store, and a street-level window display. In two weeks, the exhibit received five thousand visitors.[16]

The CIE libraries, like the American centers in other countries, did much more than furnish facilities for reading. Gradually, what began as small public libraries became community centers increasingly engaging in a wide range of popular activities including classes, exhibits, lectures, and other cultural and promotional events. Children's activities, recorded music con-

Figure 7.2. CIE Library, Tokyo.

certs, "Meet America" lectures and exhibits, democratization programs and displays were provided, plus classes in the English language, square dancing, and other educational entertainment.

OKAYAMA

The information center at Okayama is a good example. It organized a vigorous outreach program, especially shows, exhibits, and programs for children. Exhibitions of artwork by local Japanese artists and by American schoolchildren were popular. Exchanges of artwork were arranged between Japanese and American schools. Well-known Americans, including film stars and other well-known performers, were invited to appear. Violinist Yehudi Menuhin came and gave a concert. Local Japanese librarians were welcome to visit.

Fashion shows and fashion magazines were very popular. They complemented a nationwide boom in Western-style dressmaking, which quickly emerged not only as an attractive practical skill, but also as a symbol of liberation from the drab poverty and anti-Westernism of the war years.[17]

Other public relations and publicity included cocktail parties for newspaper reporters, regular weekly news releases to radio stations and newspapers, summer concerts in a city park, and a weekly posting of local events. Popular recordings were lent to the railway station to play when the trains carrying U.S. soldiers passed through in exchange for allowing the information center to make announcements during commuters' rush hours.

Programs promoted the United Nations and its agencies, notably the World Health Organization and UNESCO. About 40 percent of registered readers were students; 20 percent, technical or professional people. Most borrowing was of books in the social sciences and useful arts.[18]

Programming was quite varied. The Yokohama information center organized a "buzz session" for parents and small children. After two films, one a CIE film *Our Dream*, about an ideal children's library, the sixty children went to another room to play games while the parents heard a lecture on "how to promote a more effective family life," followed by small-group discussions and a question-and-answer session with the speaker.[19]

It is hardly surprising that these information centers were extremely popular. They also provided a vision of what public library service could be, with the novel experience of open access to the shelves, encouragement to handle books freely, and vigorous and imaginative outreach to the community.

STAFFING

Staffing the information centers was a problem, however. Suitably qualified Japanese librarians were not available, so professional librarians were imported from the United States. But ordinarily they were unfamiliar with the Japanese language and culture, so each was assigned a Japanese "adviser" who could interpret and assist in dealing with the local community. This was valuable work experience for the advisers, who generally were young, enthusiastic, and knew some English. However, the imported librarians typically wanted to return home after a year or two, necessitating recruitment of a replacement.

One grateful reader was Yukawa Hideki, who is said to have stated that a CIE information center enabled him to remain active as a physicist. He became Japan's first Nobel Laureate.

NOTES

1. Harry S. Truman, "Termination of O.W.I. and Disposition of Certain Functions of O.I.A.A. Aug 31, 1945," *Department of State Bulletin* 13, no. 323 (September 2, 1945): 306.

2. This chapter draws on John W. Gaddis, *Public Information in Japan under American Occupation: A Study of Democratization Efforts through Agencies of Public Expression* (Geneva: Imprimeries Populaires, 1950).
3. John F. Sullivan, *Information Services in Japanese Ministries. SCAP CIE Report*, December 7, 1949, quoted in Gaddis, *Public Information*, 63.
4. Gaddis, *Public Information*, 62.
5. The literature on SCAP GHQ is large. Note Takemae Eiji, *Inside GHQ: The Allied Occupation of Japan and Its Legacy* (New York: Continuum Press, 2002).
6. Gaddis, *Public Information*, 145–66: appendix A.6. See paragraph 9 (a and c), 152–53.
7. Gaddis, *Public Information*, 143–44: appendix A.5.
8. Gaddis, *Public Information*, 143–44: appendix A.5.
9. Gaddis, *Public Information*, 72.
10. Armed Services Editions. *Wikipedia*, https://en.wikipedia.org/wiki/Armed_Services_Editions.
11. For the Fleischers and the *Japan Advertiser*, see Demaree Bess, "Tokyo's Captive Yankee Newspaper," *Saturday Evening Post* 215, no. 32 (February 6, 1943): 22 and 66; and Peter O'Connor, *The English-Language Press Networks of East Asia, 1918–1945* (Folkestone: Global Oriental, 2010).
12. For Don Brown, see Yokohama Kaiko Shiryokan, *Don Buraun to Shōwa no Nihon: Korekushon de miru senji, senryō seisaku* [Don Brown and the Showa era in Japan: The war and occupation policies depending on the collection] (Yokohama-shi: Yūrindō, 2005); also, Don Brown, *Beginning of the School*. [Unedited transcript of talk given 28 November 1976]; Douglas M. Kendrick, "Don Brown," [obituary] *Transactions of the Asiatic Society of Japan*, 3rd series, 15 (1980): 1–2; and Miura Taro, "Don Buraun to sai kyouiku medeia toshiteno toshokan." [Don Brown and a library as a recurrent education medium], in Madoko Kon and Masaya Takayama, *Gendai Nihon no toshokan kōsō: sengo kaikaku to sono tenkai* (Tokyo: Bensei Shuppan, 2013), 197–212.
13. For Burnette, see "Paul J. Burnette," *Library Quarterly* 27, no. 1 (January 1957): 48; also, Madoko Kon and Masaya Takayama, *Gendai Nihon no toshokan kōsō: sengo kaikaku to sono tenkai* (Tokyo: Bensei Shuppan, 2013), 259–65; Arthur Stanionis, "Illini and the War," *Daily Illini* (March 15, 1944): 2, col. 6, http://idnc.library.illinois.edu/cgi-bin/illinois?a=d&d=DIL19440315.2.27#.
14. Hiromi Ochi, "Democratic Bookshelf: American Libraries in Occupied Japan," 89–111, in *Pressing the Fight: Print, Propaganda, and the Cold War*, edited by Greg Barnhisel and Catherine Turne (Amherst: University of Massachusetts Press, 2010); Kon Madoko, "CIE infuomeshon senta no katsudo," [The Activities of the CIE Information Center], 87–154, in Madoko Kon and Masaya Takayama, *Gendai Nihon no toshokan kōsō: sengo kaikaku to sono tenkai* (Tokyo: Bensei Shuppan, 2013).
15. Supreme Commander for the Allied Powers. *History of the Non-Military Activities of the Occupation of Japan*, 31 (Tokyo, 1950–1952): 313.
16. Arline Borer, "Japanese Marvel at Osaka Library Exhibit," *Wilson Library Bulletin* 23, no. 4 (December 1948): 310–11.
17. John W. Dower, *Embracing Defeat: Japan in the Wake of World War II* (New York: Norton, 1999), 170.
18. Details of the Okayama center are from an article by John B. McClurkin, who directed it 1950–1952: "People and Books in Japan," *Alabama Librarian*, 4 (July 1953): 18–19. See also Kon Madoko, "CIE in fuomeshon," 146–48. Other accounts of CIE information centers include F. J. Harsaghy, "Seventy Million Japanese Say 'Yes,'" *Wilson Library Bulletin* 27, no. 4 (December 1952): 309–13 and 320, also letter 27, no. 6 (February 1953): 419; Ken Kantor, "Japanese Libraries, American Style," *Wilson Library Bulletin*, 29 (September 1949): 54–55; Roland A. Mulhauser, "Information Libraries Flourish in Japan," *Library Journal*, 73 (February 1, 1948): 160–63; Ochi, "Democratic Bookshelf"; Matilda A. Roedel, "'Arigato,' Say Japanese," *Library Journal*, 74 (December 1, 1949): 1792–95 and 1806; and Supreme Commander for the Allied Powers, Civil Information and Education Section, Education Division, 1952, *Post-war Developments in Japanese Education*, vol. 1 (Tokyo, General Headquarters,

Supreme Commander for the Allied Powers, Civil Information and Education Section, Education Division): 369–71.

19. Dorothea B. Munro, "Japanese Buzz Session," *Wilson Library Bulletin* 26, no. 4 (December 1951): 326 and 330.

Chapter Eight

The Education Mission, 1946

> The tax-supported public library is another institution which fosters the spread of ideas. . . . Fortunately the roots of a public library movement in Japan already exist. . . . We visualize the organization of a great public library system for Japan . . . —Education Mission report [1]

Educational reform was fundamental and central for Allied policy, and in March 1946 an education mission of seventeen U.S. experts arrived in Japan for a month of intensive investigation and consultation. The scope of the recommendations was deliberately wide. "There is no better guarantee for democracy in Japan than a body of skilled, employed, and informed workmen," declared the mission's report submitted on March 30, 1946.[2]

OBJECTIVES

The report asserted that the Japanese educational system should be based on three objectives:

1. A system of education should be so organized as to encourage the fullest development of which individual—boy or girl, man or woman—is capable as an intelligent, responsible, and cooperating member of society. . . . Freedom of inquiry, rather than exclusive memorization of factual knowledge for examination purposes, should be emphasized.
2. The educational system has a further responsibility in the provision of types or schools or educational institutions adapted to the ability, aptitudes and interests of the students as they advance from a foundation in general education to specialized preparation for the manifold occu-

pations—agricultural, industrial, commercial, domestic, and professional—of modern society. A well-organized system of counseling and guidance, both educational and vocational, will prove useful.
3. Finally, the educational system will do well to create new interests among students, not only intellectual, but practical and esthetic. Throughout the new program, libraries and other agencies for self-education will play an important part. In fact, one of the best methods for surmounting an overemphasis on memorization of textbook or dictated materials is to provide access to books and articles representing different points of view.[3]

The political agenda was clear: "Stunned and scarred by a disastrous war caused by military domination of the masses, the Japanese are turning now toward a new battle, with peace and world cooperation as its objectives. In order to redirect the intellectual and spiritual resources of Japan, every available means should be used to effect a wide distribution of information and ideas related to human welfare." Much more was needed than efficiency and fine-tuning of a school system that was "both insular and insulated."

LEON CARNOVSKY

The membership of the education mission included Leon Carnovsky (1903–1975), then associate dean of the Graduate Library School at the University of Chicago, which was the most prestigious school of library science in the United States and for many years the only one to offer a PhD. It was established with a grant from the Carnegie Corporation in a conscious attempt to transform professional education for librarians.

Leon Carnovsky had studied philosophy and sociology and then, after brief experience working in a public library and in a university library, was an early PhD graduate of the Chicago graduate library school with a dissertation on students' reading interests. He stayed on as a faculty member from 1932 to 1971. Carnovsky had wide interests, but he specialized in the role of library services in society, and he conducted several surveys of public libraries. Carnovsky wrote the parts of the mission's report concerned with library services. He also directed a program by which members of the mission paid for the purchase of books, which were placed on display in one of Tokyo's largest department stores, then sent to various teachers' training institutions before being distributed to selected schools.[4]

PHILIP KEENEY

CIE provided administrative support to the mission and extensive assistance. Carnovsky had discussions with CIE's library specialist, Philip Olin Keeney (1891–1962), known to his friends as Angus. Keeney had a certificate in librarianship from Berkeley's School of Librarianship, had worked at the University of Michigan libraries, and then became university librarian and professor of library science at Montana State University in Missoula. Unfortunately, his improvements in library service, praised in a subsequent survey of the library, were overshadowed by increasing conflict over intellectual freedom and academic tenure with two successive tyrannical university presidents.

Keeney was a left-leaning progressive in a conservative environment, so some conflict was predictable. Among his reforms he established an openly accessible collection of recreational reading for undergraduates, which he called The Open Shelf. It included a novel by a local author, Vardis Fisher, titled *Passions Spin the Plot*, about a selfish, unpleasant college student who treats everybody badly, including his fiancée, especially after he learns that she had had more sexual experience than he had. The book depicts unethical behavior, but it has no obscene content. However, a complaint about this book caused the university president to demand its removal and the summary dismissal of Keeney even though he had a tenured appointment. Keeney sued, and with help from the American Federation of Teachers, the American Civil Liberties Union, and the Association of American University Professors, he won reinstatement ordered by the Montana Supreme Court. This victory became an important legal precedent for academic tenure, but Keeney had become ill, his position was in practice untenable, and he resigned.

The American Library Association, then a rather conservative organization, had not helped Keeney. Largely as a result of his experience, he and others founded a Progressive Librarians' Council intended to make the association more democratic, to promote federal and state funding for libraries, and "to unite all progressive librarians whose single voices are inaudible into a group which will be heard."[5]

After a couple of years unemployed in Berkeley, Keeney moved to Washington, DC, where he worked in a series of positions in the federal government including the Library of Congress, the Office of Strategic Services, and the State Department.

At the end of 1945 he accepted a nine-month assignment to conduct social research in Japan, where he was assigned to the government section of the general headquarters of SCAP, where he was on the committee developing the local government aspects of the draft constitution and looked after a library. Then, in February 1946, he transferred to the education division of the civil information and education section, where he began to attend to library services in Japan and, just in time, to assist Carnovsky. In July he was promoted and designated library officer.[6]

The staffing pattern within CIE comprised a range of specialists, all of whom were expected to formulate policies and plans within their assigned field, engage in consultation within SCAP and with Japanese, and eventually propose courses of action to be implemented by the Japanese government with SCAP's advice and assistance as necessary.

LIBRARY RECOMMENDATIONS

In the education mission's report concerning primary and secondary education, school libraries merit little mention beyond "there should be provided an adequate supply of text and reference books, library books, and other instructional equipment. Visual and aural aids to instruction should be available for use more extensively than has heretofore been true."[7] It also voiced a concern for more and better books for children.

Because Japan had more adults than children, the task of adult education required attention, and almost half of chapter 5 on adult education is a plea for a tax-supported public library with branches "serving all communities" with no fees for use or for borrowing. "The tax-supported public library is another institution which fosters the spread of ideas," the report states; and, "Fortunately the roots of a public library movement in Japan already exist. Municipal and prefectural libraries in considerable numbers flourished throughout the nation, but most of these were partially or totally destroyed. It should recalled, however, that the library system, although public was not free. There was usually an admission fee and a charge was made for borrowing books."

The report visualizes the organization of "a great public library system for Japan" that "fosters the spread of ideas" and "is an ever welcome source of cultural refreshment."

> The Ministry of Education would have a director of public library service whose function would be to help the libraries throughout the nation by publishing booklists and bibliographies and by advising on library administrative matters. He would be responsible for the distribution of funds made available by the national government. He might also establish standards for libraries. In each city and prefecture there would be a chief librarian appointed locally or by the prefectural government. Each library would have branch collections in schools, book stations in community buildings and would provide special service to outlying areas.[8]

Recognizing the high cost and ambitious nature of this sweeping program, the education mission recommended starting with an experimental library program in Tokyo as a testing ground and a model.

Universities in Japan had followed German patterns rather than British or American, and this was reflected in their libraries: multiple, separate autonomous departmental collections jealously controlled by autocratic professors, a relatively weak central library usually directed by a professor lacking professional credentials, an absence of coordination, and little respect for professional qualifications. This background needs to be emphasized in order to appreciate the mission's library recommendations, which followed standard U.S. practices:

> Essential for research and for the development of the individual student on all levels of higher education is the library.
> To make available to all students the resources of the country, we suggest that each university consider unifying and consolidating its collections, preparing a single union catalogue. These, together with similar catalogues of collections of learned societies, might be incorporated in a master union catalog to be maintained at some central agency. Thus might be achieved the basis of a national bibliography that would be of inestimable value to scholars in locating the books they want.
> A system of inter-library loans should be instituted within Japan, and, as soon as possible, a system of international exchange which prevailed before the war should be resumed.
> It would be useful, we think, for the university libraries of Japan to organize a professional association. A library school might also well be established preferably affiliated with a university that has good library facilities, in order to train professional personnel.[9]

These recommendations may now appear routine, even timid, but in the context and at that time they implied radical change. Soon after the education mission left Japan, Keeney submitted his own plan for a unified library plan for Japan.

NOTES

1. United States, Education Mission to Japan, *Report of the United States Education Mission to Japan. Submitted to the Supreme Commander for the Allied Powers, Tokyo, March 30, 1946* (Washington, DC: U.S. Government Printing Office, 1946), 45, https://catalog.hathitrust.org/Record/011325745.
2. United States, Education Mission, *Report*, 18.
3. United States, Education Mission, *Report*, 19
4. For Carnovsky, see William C. Heygood, "Leon Carnovsky: A Sketch," *Library Quarterly* 38, no. 4 (October 1968): 422–28; *Toshokan jōhōgaku kyōiku no sengoshi: shiryō ga kataru senmonshoku yōsei seido no tenkai* [The Postwar History of Library and Information Science Education: The Development of Professional Training System Based on Materials], edited by Nemoto Akira (Kyoto: Mineruva Shobō, 2015), 4 and 936; Frederick A. Schlipf,

"Leon Carnovsky: A Bibliography," *Library Quarterly*, 38 (October 1968): 429–41; Howard Winger, "Carnovsky, Leon (1903–1975)," 73–74, in *Dictionary of American Library Biography*, edited by Bohdan. S. Wynar (Littleton, CO: Libraries Unlimited, 1978).

5. Rosalee McReynolds and Louise S. Robbins, *The Librarian Spies: Philip and Mary Jane Keeney and Cold War Espionage* (Westport, CT: Praeger, 2009) is a joint biography of Keeney and his wife. For Keeney's library achievements at the University of Montana, see Maurice F. Tauber and Eugene H. Wilson, *Report of a Survey of the Library of Montana State University for Montana State University, January–May 1951* (Chicago: American Library Association, 1951), 20, http://hdl.handle.net/2027/mdp.39015034609811. For his conflict over book selection, see also Rosalee McReynolds, "Trouble in Big Sky's Ivory Tower: The Montana Tenure Dispute of 1937–1939," *Libraries and Culture*, 32 (Spring 1997): 163–90; Joe W. Kraus, "The Progressive Librarians Council," *Library Journal*, 97 (July 1972): 2351–54. See also discussion of the Library Law in chapter 11.

6. Theodore McNelly, *Origins of Japan's Democratic Constitution* (Lanham, MD: University Press of America, 2000), 66–67. Keeney reported on his library work and experiences in Japan in four articles: "Japanese Librarians are War-Damaged," *Library Journal*, 73 (May 1, 1948): 681–84; "Meet the Japanese Librarians," *Library Journal*, 73 (May 15, 1948): 768–72; "Reorganization of the Japanese Library System," *Far Eastern Survey*, 17 (January 28, 1948): 19–22; and (February 11, 1948): 32–35. The last two are reprinted with other memoranda in *Toshokanhō seiritsushi shiryō*, edited by Takeo Urata and Ogawa Takeshi (Tokyo: Nihon Toshokan Kyōkai, 1968), 419–33. McReynolds and Robbins, *Librarian Spies*, briefly covers his library work in Japan. The University of Berkeley Bancroft Library has a collection of his papers: *Philip Olin Keeney Papers*, BANC MSS 71/157.

7. United States, Education Mission, *Report*, 30
8. United States, Education Mission, *Report*, 40.
9. United States, Education Mission, *Report*, 54.

Chapter Nine

Keeney and His Plan

> One method of meeting these needs is to organize the surviving libraries of Japan into a national system along the lines of the California Library System.
> —Philip Keeney, 1946

KEENEY IN CALIFORNIA

Philip Keeney, the CIE library specialist who had assisted Leon Carnovsky with the library aspects of the education mission's report, would have been very familiar with the California county library system described in chapter 4. Ill health had caused him to drop out of a degree in chemistry at MIT in 1915. He went west to work outdoors in sunny California in the Orland Irrigation Project, a reclamation area one hundred miles north of Sacramento. The Orland project, centered in Glenn County, also included parts of Colusa and Tehama counties, and has an unusually pleasant climate. The bookish Keeney would have been well aware of the introduction of free public library services in these three counties in 1914, 1915, and 1916, respectively.[1]

In 1924 Keeney left farming and joined his two sisters who were now also in California, living in Berkeley. The city had no public library until 1893 when 264 donated books were made available. By the time Keeney arrived, excellent public library service had been developed. Carleton B. Joeckel, the city librarian from 1914 to 1927, was from Wisconsin, where he had been inspired by the progressive social policies of the governor, Robert M. LaFollette. Joeckel went to fight on the Western Front in World War I, and he returned as Captain Joeckel, a wounded war hero. Inspired by the effectiveness of military administration, he became the leading authority nationally on public library governance and built up Berkeley's public library with a large, central main library and four branches, the pattern that continues today a century later.

At Berkeley Keeney enrolled at the University of California. His interests had changed from chemistry to history. He completed his bachelor's degree in 1925 in history, after which he enrolled in Berkeley's library school and completed his certificate in librarianship in 1927. At the library school, Keeney would have been in close contact with its director, Sydney Mitchell, whom he later referred to as "my old Mentor."[2] Keeney would also have had close contact with Carleton Joeckel, who taught part-time and later served as a reference for him. Given this formative environment, it is not surprising that Keeney worked for years on a scholarly book titled "Librarianship: A Social Force." It was never published and probably was never finished. No surviving manuscript is known, but part of it appeared as an article titled "The Public Library: A People's University?" in the *Wilson Library Bulletin* in 1938 with a strongly supportive comment by the editor.[3]

The California county library system would have been very familiar to all students in the Berkeley School of Librarianship in which California State Library staff regularly taught. It is very likely that he knew Harriet Eddy, who at that time lived in Berkeley and worked on the Berkeley campus as an agricultural extension agent.

A UNIFIED PLAN

After arriving in Japan to conduct social research in SCAP's government section, Keeney transferred to the Civil Information and Education section (CIE) and became the library specialist in the education division, where he assisted Leon Carnovsky with the library recommendations of the education mission report.

That report finally was completed on March 30, 1946. A few days later, Philip Keeney, probably encouraged by the education mission's recommendations concerning libraries and by his discussions with Leon Carnovsky, submitted a strategic plan for the overall development of library services in Japan to his supervisor, Edward H. Farr. Titled *Unified Library Service for Japan*, the plan was quite short—less than fifteen hundred words including suggested procedures for implementation. It is reprinted in full in this book's appendix. Keeney's transmittal note to Farr, dated April 8, 1946, noted:

> The accompanying study for a Unified Library Service for Japan is the result of several conversations with Mr. Carnovsky when he was in Tokyo with the Education Mission and informal talks with several Japanese librarians. Its basic principles are similar to the California County Library System which has been used, in part, by many other states in the United States and several foreign countries. . . . A free public library movement is considered an impor-

tant factor in advancing the democratic idea, hence any project supporting free libraries, which Japan has never had, at least according to American standards, seems to be of vital importance now.

The first section of Keeney's plan described the need. The second section addressed the solution in two parts: the immediate opening of such libraries as could be opened and "a long-range program for pooling all the library resources in Japan into a single, unified system."[4] It noted,

> One method of meeting these needs is to organize the surviving libraries of Japan into a national system along the lines of the California Library System, which makes available, by means of inter-library loans by mail, the entire resources of the State to every citizen. Adopted in California in 1911, the system has been found to offer the widest library service to the greatest number of people at the least cost.

Keeney noted that Japan was similar in size to California, that the national library at Ueno Park could act like the California State Library, and that "the prefectural libraries correspond closely to, and already carry on some of the same functions as, the county libraries of California."[5]

The plan concisely echoes the characteristics of the California county library system with its emphasis on coordination. The purpose was simply stated:

> The aim is to create a library system which will be (1) unified; (2) economical, available to all localities on an equal basis, and complete; (3) organized as an integral part of the total educational system, co-ordinate with the classroom; (4) available to adults studying outside the classroom.

The plan argued that because only large units were capable of supporting a range of quality services, the logical unit would be the prefecture (or a regional group of prefectures) with service delivered through branch libraries in local communities or reading rooms within local institutions. The librarians in charge of each unit should be professionally qualified. The prefectural or regional services would be linked to the national library, which, like the California State Library, would maintain a union catalog to facilitate interlibrary loans at no charge to the reader.

The postwar development of Japan, Keeney wrote, depends on providing adult education to enable people to apply all kinds of knowledge to their various tasks. Remedial support will be needed by some who previously lacked opportunities for education. Those whose education has been adequate will need to have their knowledge continually brought up to date in the fields related to their occupations. A unified library system can be organized as a channel for such knowledge and delivered to even the smallest community. This will require some coordination so that all may share in the total collection of books throughout an organized area. Thus, the aim is to create a library system that will be act as a coherent whole.

A unit large enough to provide adequately and efficiently the usual service and to employ a trained librarian, such as a county in California, could provide better, more cost-effective service than individual villages operating separately. The logical unit for public library administration in Japan would be the prefecture (or a group of prefectures organized into a region) and headquartered in the principal city but with service provided in a decentralized way to the local communities.

A trained librarian should be in charge as soon as library schools have candidates to recommend. Each headquarters library would be a clearinghouse for a library service in every community in that prefecture or region, with branches established wherever needed to reach every resident. Existing public libraries should be incorporated, and branches located within existing accessible institutions (schools, community centers, etc.) should be established as needed.

A qualified chief librarian would visit the communities, employ local custodians, and ensure the presence of books, magazines, and other material useful for each community's needs and purposes. Little-used materials would be replaced and repurposed. Other material, when wanted, would be obtained from the regional headquarters or elsewhere.

Each prefectural or regional organization would cooperate with the national library, which would maintain a union catalog of all books in Japanese libraries in order to make them available through interlibrary loan at no cost to the reader. A national union catalog listing books, periodicals, and, selectively, maps, globes, pictures, films, and other resources, is necessary for filling special requests and to avoid spending money unnecessarily on duplicative acquisitions. Thus, Keeney wrote, using capital letters for emphasis:

> Thus no matter where one lives, he has access to all the library service within Japan making the service EQUAL; all library material is used as far as possible, making the service ECONOMICAL; every possibility of filling a request is resorted to, making the service COMPLETE; and every unit of service—the already established public library, the school library, the prefectural and national libraries—is woven into one system making it completely UNIFIED.

Keeney noted that such a plan had been carried out in varying degrees of completeness in different parts of the United States and in other countries, and that it would be especially suitable for Japan given the destruction of libraries and other means of education. Presumably, he intended that this document would build on the impetus of the education mission's recommendations and provide the basis for building a policy consensus within CIE and then acceptance by SCAP, which would be needed for any significant official move. Donald Nugent, who became head of CIE two months later, in June

1946, was born and educated in California. He, too, would have been familiar with the California county library system.

Keeney added detailed suggestions for consultation and planning. A top-down approach by the ministry would have been procedurally necessary in the circumstances in Japan at that time, but Keeney was deeply committed to consultative and participatory approaches to management that he had advocated repeatedly in articles in the professional journals.[6]

KEENEY AS LIBRARY OFFICER

The role of a CIE specialist was to advise and assist, and Keeney's efforts were exemplary. He made many visits in and beyond Tokyo and he consulted widely, not only with Japanese librarians and educators but also with SCAP military government officials who, until early 1947, were placed in each prefecture to facilitate the implementation of new policies. Keeney consulted librarians, visited libraries, and talked with educators and local officials. He tried to get library buildings that had been taken over for other purposes restored to library use, new premises assigned, or old ones refurbished. In July 1946 he was promoted and given the title library officer.

Keeney made a point of promoting the status of women in librarianship. He urged that the Ueno Imperial Library "act for all Japanese libraries as the California State Library acts for county libraries in California." Mark T. Orr took over from E. H. Farr as head of the education division in September 1946, and Keeney reported on his work in memoranda to him.[7] After one trip he wrote, "Though this trip was arduous, undersigned feels that the contact made with M[ilitary] G[overnment] teams, Japanese librarians, and many prefectural education officials were exceedingly profitable and will bear fruit in the library field."[8]

A high point in Keeney's work was his role in a conference of Japanese librarians sponsored by the Ministry of Education in Tokyo August 15–17, 1946, at the Ueno Imperial Library to discuss a proposed new public library law. Afterward, he reported to Orr:[9]

> The undersigned described certain American library laws with particular emphasis on the Library of Congress and the California County Library System. . . . On the second night of the conference, the undersigned invited the visiting librarians, Mombusho [Ministry of Education] officials and several Tokyo librarians to dine at the Dai Ichi. During the dinner there was a continued flow of friendly conversation pertaining to librarianship. . . . It really was a festive occasion affording all the diners an excellent opportunity to become better acquainted with each other. . . . It was obvious the dinner sparked the rest of the conference, for a committee of twelve librarians worked nearly all of Friday night preparing the final version of the text of the new legislation.

Figure 9.1. Philip Keeney in Japan.

The Dai Ichi building was occupied by SCAP general headquarters, and Japanese were ordinarily excluded. The dinner that Keeney arranged there was without precedent, and his guests greatly appreciated it.

In addition to working with Carnovsky on the education mission, Keeney also worked with Mae Graham, an experienced school librarian and educator of school librarians who spent months at CIE in 1947 as a consultant on school libraries. She collaborated with Japanese librarians in the development for the ministry of education of a guide for school libraries. She also conducted an extended workshop in the Institutes for Educational Leadership (IFEL) series.

Consistent with his long-established insistence on consultative management and inclusion, he organized conferences of librarians. One was for librarians of private universities held in July 1946. Another meeting, claimed to be "Japan's first national conference of librarians from all types of libraries," was held in August 1946 and noted above. The delegates spent three days developing plans and policies, including draft legislation on salaries and civil service rank, drafted a new constitution for the Japan Library Association, explored possibilities for increased financial support, and planned for the revival of library training at the Ueno Imperial Library but with a broader professional curriculum and higher criteria for admission. In the fall, the new constitution of the Japan Library Association transforming it into a modern professional association was adopted by a majority vote of the members. Sydney Mitchell, who stressed the role of professional associations and of consultation, would have been pleased. Figure 9.2 shows Keeney with a group of librarians of Imperial university libraries.[10]

WILLOUGHBY AND "LEFTIES"

Charles Willoughby, who had served during the war as MacArthur's head of military intelligence, accompanied MacArthur to Tokyo, where he also acquired additional responsibility for civilian counterintelligence and supervision of police. Willoughby, a German who had adopted his English mother's surname and become a naturalized U.S. citizen, had very conservative political views. He admired the Fascist regime in Spain and later went to work for its leader, General Francisco Franco. Willoughby was suited to the emerging anti-Communism of the Cold War. Communists, Trotskyites, and Socialists, even progressive thinkers opposed to Soviet Communism, were lumped together by him as "lefties," and Willoughby enthusiastically made long lists of suspected lefties. He was determined to expel them all as subversives, and he complained when his staff did not find incriminating evidence. Willoughby wrongly accused Canadian diplomat Herbert Norman of being a Communist spy and, among numerous others, denounced Keeney as a "known communist and courier."[11]

The paranoia of the Red Scare period was illustrated when Keeney's wife, Mary Jane, sent a small folding umbrella to him. Instead of sending it by mail, she asked a SCAP employee who was returning from the United States to Tokyo to take it for her. The employee did, but proudly reported later in her reminiscences that she had reported the request to the Federal Bureau of Investigation as suspicious.[12]

Figure 9.2. Conference of librarians of imperial universities, 1946. Front row from left: Akashi Sadayuki, Hokkaido; Sakurai Tadashi, Kyushu; Omodaka Hisataka, Kyoto; Takahashi Yutaka, Tohoyu; Philip Keeney; Ichikawa Sanki, Tokyo; Sugita Naoki, Nagoya; Shimizu Tatsujiro, Osaka. Second row: Takeda Susumu, Hokkaida; Kochi Hideo, Hokkaida; Shigahisa Tokutaro, Tohoku; Miyanishi Mitsuo, Kyoto; Mizuno Akira, Tokyo; Tanaka Kei, Osaka; Doi Shigeyoshi, Tokyo; Kawai Hiroshi, Tokyo; Aono Iyoji, Tokyo. Back row: Nakae Toshiro, Kyushu; Yagyu Shiro, Tokyo; Oshima Takeshiro, Nagoya.

Keeney had strongly held progressive, left-wing views. He supported labor unions, consultative management, and freedom of speech. Anybody with Keeney's views would have been a target for Willoughby. A year after submitting his unified plan for Japanese libraries, Keeney was suddenly arrested, apparently as a suspected security risk. It was not a new accusation. In 1942, when Keeney worked at the Library of Congress, J. Edgar Hoover, director of the Federal Bureau of Investigation, had demanded that the librarian of Congress, Archibald MacLeish, dismiss Keeney as a subversive. MacLeish refused after his administrative assistant, Verner Clapp, investigated and found no evidence and Hoover, when challenged, supplied none.[13]

Don Brown also was caught up in the Red Scare and was dismissed as a subversive in 1954. Brown managed to achieve reinstatement several months later.[14] Keeney was less fortunate. He received a "notice of separation" on April 22, 1947, and was sent back to the United States. Japanese librarians and his CIE supervisor, Mark T. Orr, wrote testimonials praising Keeney's work in the strongest terms. Nevertheless, on June 9, 1947, Keeney was relieved of duties and discharged without explanation.

Keeney's fate and the fate of Keeney's plan will be taken up later. But first came a very important development relating to the national legislature, the Diet, and another American mission.

NOTES

1. For Keeney in Japan, see Rosalee McReynolds and Louise S. Robbins, *The Librarian Spies: Philip and Mary Jane Keeney and Cold War Espionage* (Westport, CT: Praeger, 2009), 91–97; Theodore McNelly, *Origins of Japan's Democratic Constitution* (Lanham, MD: University Press of America, 2000), 66–68.

2. Philip O. Keeney to Paul North Rice, July 16, 1937, Keeney Papers, Bancroft Library, Box 1:12.

3. Philip O. Keeney, "The Public Library: A People's University?" *Wilson Library Bulletin* 13, no. 6 (February 1939): 369–77 and 387.

4. Keeney's fullest account appeared as "Reorganization of the Japanese Library System," *Far Eastern Survey*, 17 (January 28, 1948): 19–22 and (February 11, 1948): 32–35, reprinted in *Toshokanhō seiritsushi shiryō*, edited by Takeo Urata and Takeshi Ogawa (Tokyo: Nihon Toshokan Kyokai, 1968), 419–33.

5. Keeney, "Reorganization," 33.

6. For example, Philip O. Keeney, "Democratic Aids to Staff Responsibility," *Library Journal* 59, no. 12 (April 15, 1934): 361; "Against Autocratic Library Management," *Library Journal* 59, no. 11 (April 1, 1934): 312–13; and "The Responsibility of Being Head Librarian," *Library Journal* 59, no. 6 (March 15, 1934): 271–72.

7. Some or all of eight of these memos are reprinted in Urata and Ogawa, *Toshokanhō*, 438–57. Copies of the originals are in Keeney Papers, Bancroft, box 2:1.

8. Memo, Keeney to Mark T. Orr, April 3, 1947, Keeney papers, Box 2:1; Urata and Ogawa, *Toshokanhō*, 436–37.

9. Memo, Keeney to Orr, September 1, 1946, Keeney papers, Box 2:1; Urata and Ogawa, *Toshokanhō*, 438–41.

10. Two other conference group photos of Keeney with Japanese librarians are in Philip Keeney, "Meet the Japanese Librarians," *Library Journal*, 73 (May 15, 1948): 769 and 771.

11. Roger Bowen, *Innocence Is Not Enough: The Life and Death of Herbert Norman* (Armonk, NY: M. E. Sharpe, 1986), 220–21; John W. Dower, *Embracing Defeat: Japan in the Wake of World War II* (New York: Norton, 1999); McNelly, *Origins*, 66–68; Takemae Eiji, *Inside GHQ: The Allied Occupation of Japan and Its Legacy* (New York: Continuum, 2002), 161–62.

12. Eleanor M. Hadley, *Memoir of a Trustbuster: A Lifelong Adventure with Japan*, with P. H. Kuwayama (Honolulu: University of Hawaii Press, 2003), 122–23.

13. Clapp to Keeney, December 7, 1942. Keeney Papers, box 1:12,

14. *GHQ Jōhō Kachō Don Buraun to sono jidai: Shōwa no Nihon to Amerika* [Don Brown as the Chief of Information Division of GHQ and the Era], Yokohama Kokusai Kankeishi Kenkyūkai, Yokohama Kaikō Shiryōkan hen (Tokyo: Nihon Keizai Hyoronsha, 2009), 102.

Chapter Ten

The National Diet Library

> We agreed that no two librarians ever before had such an opportunity to bring the rich experience of one country to the assistance of another where conditions appeared to be ripe to profit from it. After five weeks in Japan we are still of that mind. —Verner W. Clapp, 1948

THE IMPERIAL LIBRARY

James Gillis had transformed the California State Library from a large but passive collection into an active agency promoting and supporting library services across the state. This new role involved not only outreach and encouragement, but also active leadership in developing legislation, funding, and practical amenities ("infrastructure") that libraries need to have available in order to provide good service but could not provide for themselves. Examples included access to official documents, a union catalog, a bibliographical index to California publications, expert advisers, and even, for a while, a training program to meet the acute shortage of librarians. In effect, the California State Library had changed from a large, passive collection to an active state library agency. Other state libraries in America were making the same move.

Similarly, from the end of the nineteenth century national libraries around the world gradually were following the same path. The Library of Congress started to make copies of its catalog records available to other libraries to reduce the cost of local cataloging. In Britain and France, the national libraries undertook ambitious projects to make their catalogs available in printed book form as a monumental bibliographical resource. Other concerns were the development of national, even international, standard cataloging rules and, especially, complete bibliographies of works published in (or about) a country. Progress varied greatly from country to country, especially until UNESCO, founded in 1946, made universal adoption of comprehensive bibliographic infrastructure and standards a significant and influential part of its program. Overall, it was a critical transition from passive library collections toward agencies actively advancing libraries and library service.

The Japanese government had established a large library under the Ministry of Education in 1872. In 1890, known as the Imperial Library, it was designated the national library of Japan, and a new building was erected for it in Tokyo's Ueno Park. A training institute for librarians, started in 1922, moved into the library in 1925, but by 1945, there had otherwise been little movement in Japan from a national collection to a national agency advancing library services. Independently, the League of Young Librarians (Seinen Toshokan'in Rehmei), led by Mamiya Fujio, had taken the initiative to provide some useful manuals.

FAHS'S PROPOSAL

Early in 1946, and probably independent of the education mission and Keeney's efforts, Charles Burton Fahs proposed that SCAP arrange for experts to visit Japan to make recommendations for the strategic development of a national library. Dr. Fahs was important for two reasons. First, he was a senior official concerned with Far Eastern issues at the State Department. Second, he was one of the few American experts on Japan, and he had a reputation for a realistic, factual understanding of the Japanese economy and politics.

Charles Burton Fahs (1908–1980) had received an MA and a PhD in international studies at Northwestern University specializing in the Far East. He spent a year studying at Kyoto Imperial University and another year at Tokyo Imperial University. In 1936 he joined Pomona College in Claremont, California, to teach Oriental studies. In 1940 he published a study of government practices in Japan, and in 1941 he left to become a research analyst in the federal Office of the Coordinator of Information and then in the Office of Strategic Services, 1942–1945, where he became chief of the Far East division, 1944–1945. He then became acting chief of the division for research on the Far East in the Department of State, 1945–1946. The son of a librarian, Fahs had a significant interest in library services.[1]

LEGISLATIVE SUPPORT FOR THE NATIONAL DIET

The new constitution, finally approved on November 3, 1946, took effect on May 3, 1947. A central feature was the greatly increased the role of the Diet, making it "the highest organ of State power" and "the sole law-making organ of the State." Previously, the emperor had been the source of law, and the Cabinet had handled preparation of legislation. The role of the Imperial Diet, composed of a House of Representatives and a House of Peers, was to approve legislation prepared by the government in the Cabinet office.

Under the new constitution, the National Diet assumed much greater responsibilities, but it was ill-equipped to perform its new role. Members of the Diet would need significant support staff, including reliable information services. A memorandum by Justin Williams of SCAP's government section, dated September 1946, had made fourteen recommendations—including recommendation 6, that a Diet library be established; and recommendation 7, that each house have adequate legislative reference service. The National Diet Law provided that "a Diet Library shall be attached to the Diet in order to help members of the Diet conduct their investigations and researches" and that "the use of the Diet Library may be extended to the general public." These provisions were incorporated in the subsequent Diet Library Law of March 1947.[2]

Library service for legislative bodies normally is separate from the work of a national library. But deliberations concerning the needs of the new Diet library recognized that Japan lacked the bibliographic infrastructure and interlibrary cooperation ordinarily arranged by a modern national library. The new Diet Library, no matter how well equipped in itself, could never hope to function with full effectiveness as long as such services were lacking in Japan; nor, as Keeney might have pointed out, could other libraries in Japan, absent both a modern national library *and* a unified national plan for Japanese libraries. These discussions led to a proposal that the Diet Library itself should accept responsibility for performing national library functions. It would be more practical, given the shortage of resources, to develop a single library—both to serve as national library and to provide library service to the Diet—rather than to attempt parallel development of a National Library and a separate Diet Library.

In July 1947 leaders of the two houses of the Diet asked MacArthur to provide experts to assist in planning a single National and Diet Library. SCAP intended a three-member team: a member of the Library of Congress staff, an expert on university libraries, and an expert on public libraries. However, recruitment proved difficult, and to avoid delay a mission of just two experts was sent: Verner Clapp of the Library of Congress, as chair, and Charles Harvey Brown, the librarian at Iowa State College.[3]

VERNER CLAPP AND CHARLES HARVEY BROWN

Verner Warren Clapp (1901–1972) was born in Johannesburg, South Africa, to an American father and a mother of Danish descent who brought him to the United States in 1905. After earning his BA, he got a temporary post as a cataloger in the manuscript division of the Library of Congress. Then, after a year of graduate study of philosophy at Harvard, he returned to the Library of Congress as a reference assistant and stayed for more than thirty years. In 1928 he was assigned responsibility for a new unit to provide information service to members of Congress. This unit became the highly respected Congressional Reference Service. Clapp's wide interests, breadth of knowledge, and administrative ability led to a variety of special assignments, including wartime protective measures for the most valuable items in the collections, developing regional lending libraries of books for the blind, and establishing the United Nations library. He rose steadily through the ranks to become deputy librarian of Congress and, briefly, acting librarian of Congress. In 1947 he had been promoted from director of the acquisitions department to chief assistant librarian. Clapp was exceptionally well qualified for this mission to advise on the National Diet Library.[4]

Charles Harvey Brown (1875–1960) was a specialist in the literature of science and technology. He had recently retired after twenty-four years as the

Figure 10.1. Verner Clapp.

librarian of the Iowa State College of Agricultural and Mechanic Arts, now Iowa State University. Trained in mathematics as well as librarianship, he is remembered for his leadership in professional associations and a quantitative analysis of scientific serials.[5] A former president of the American Library Association, he was tall, elderly, conservative, and autocratic. He was opposed to staff participation in decision making and to women in administration. In that, his views were very different from Philip Keeney's, but by this time Keeney had been sent back to the United States.[6]

Clapp and Brown set off for Japan in early December 1947. At Fairfield-Suisun Army Air Base in California, the main departure point for military flights to the Far East, now Travis Air Force Base, they had to wait for four days for available seats. This provided a good opportunity to discuss and to plan their two-month assignment to make recommendations concerning the development of a National Library. They were very aware of their extraordinary opportunity to make an important and enduring contribution. "We agreed that no two librarians ever before had such an opportunity to bring the rich experience of one country to the assistance of another where conditions appeared to be ripe to profit from it. After five weeks in Japan we are still of that mind," wrote Clapp on his return.[7]

After arrival in Japan on December 14, 1947, they found that much of the necessary work had already been done by Diet committees, other interested bodies, and by staff of the CIE section of SCAP, where Paul Burnette now served as CIE's library officer.

The U.S. Library of Congress is exceptional in combining library service to the legislature with the role of national library. However, the fact that experts from the United States recommended that Japan should follow the same pattern as the United States should not be regarded as showing lack of imagination. First-rate library service to the Diet needed the kind of infrastructure and services ordinarily provided by a national library in the form of bibliographies of national publications, standardized cataloging practices, extensive research collections to supplement local collections, a union catalog of many libraries' holdings, supervision of a system of interlibrary loan, and, in general, the kind of leadership and coordination that James Gillis had implemented in California. But these important features of national library service were largely lacking in Japan. A single strategic development would be more affordable and more cost-effective than separate initiatives to develop library service for the Diet and a national library service separately.

After extensive consultations, Clapp and Brown drafted their report and then went to visit projects in China while their recommendations were discussed in Tokyo.

Their recommendations followed the emerging best practices of the time. For example, responsibility for acquisitions was firmly divided between two different departments: one concerned with selection, deciding what should be acquired; and the other concerned with accessions, the practical procedures for obtaining, through purchase, exchange, donation, or legally mandated deposit, copies of what the other department had selected. The resulting design did follow the structure of the Library of Congress but with a large difference: the National Diet Library also was made responsible for numerous libraries serving all agencies of the national government.

Clapp and Brown, like Keeney, emphasized the need for a unified approach to library services. The first chapter of their report was titled *A National Library Service for Japan* and it noted the need for a national library

> to perform services of a kind that can be most efficiently rendered on a national basis to assist in making the informational and cultural resources of the nation available to its entire people. Lacking these services, no library, however well equipped it may be individually, can hope to function with full effectiveness; with them, even the smallest library can take its place in a national system whose unity is derived not from administrative authority but from participation in common methods of work and in common knowledge of sources of information. An adequate national library system is consequently not only an essential instrument for the efficient employment of national information resources, but also is a potent engine of democracy. Its effect is to make available to all what would otherwise be reserved to the few; to put the possessions of the nation genuinely at the service of all its citizens.[8]

After noting the advantages of collaboration and standardization, they continued:

> The people of Japan are great users of books, and there are copious evidences that they would derive great benefits from adequate library facilities. Their lack of such facilities can be traced in large part to the deficiency of basic national library services, and this in turn to the prevailing political philosophy, which, in the case of the Diet, made its members almost completely dependent for information upon the executive branch of the Government. In suggesting the following functions and organization for the National Diet Library, therefore, the Library Mission has considered, first, the needs of the Diet members themselves; next the needs of the National Government in all its branches; and, throughout, the service of the nation as a whole.[9]

The second chapter listed ten objectives and functions, starting with reference and research services for all members of the Diet "to aid them with factual information in the determination of policies." The final section of the report bluntly addressed the shortage of trained librarians:

> Librarians with adequate education and experience are extremely rare in Japan today. It will be impossible to find persons in the immediate future who will be fully qualified to fill positions in the National Diet Library.... Many hundreds of trained librarians will be needed annually in Japan.[10]

Some short-term measures such as training institutes, leaves of absence to study abroad, and the temporary appointment of underqualified staff were suggested, but clearly more was needed. "A definite program for the education of men and women for librarianship should be outlined during 1948." The Library Training Institute at Ueno Park had been revived as a two-year program, but was believed to have only ten students. Clapp and Brown thought it should be developed and possibly administered in conjunction with a university. However, the Ueno Institute remained small, graduating only twelve students in 1950. The low status and uncompetitive salaries of librarians were seen as obstacles.

After extensive consultation, a National Diet Library bill was introduced on February 4, and it was immediately and unanimously approved by both chambers. A separate bill establishing a National Diet Library Building Commission also was approved. The formal report by Clapp and Brown, titled *Report of the United States Library Mission to Advise on the Establishment of the National Diet Library of Japan*, was issued on February 8, 1948. In it, they modestly insisted that their role had been "merely catalytic—it has only assisted in the formulation of ideas and purposes which existed before its arrival in Japan." They praised the "excellent teamwork between the Diet Committees and the officials of the Japanese Government and of GHQ, SCAP."[11]

KANAMORI TOKUJIRO AND NAKAI MASAKAZU

Promptly on February 7, 1948, the appointment of Kanamori Tokujiro as director of the new library was announced. In 1924, Kanamori had been appointed director of the new Cabinet Legislation Bureau, where new legislation was drafted. After being pressured to resign because his ideas were considered too secular, he became a respected constitutional scholar. He re-entered politics after the surrender and handled negotiations with SCAP concerning the new constitution adopted in 1946. He was a watercolor painter, an expert on alpine botany, and had a reputation for integrity.[12]

There had been conflict over the choice of director. There was another candidate, Nakai Masakazu, who had had an unusual career. After deep engagement with Pure Lands Buddhism, which favors a practical view of life, he had read German philosophy extensively, adopted Socialist (but not Marxist) ideas, and taught aesthetics in the philosophy department at Kyoto Imperial University until dismissed in 1937 for his leftist opposition to Fascism. He was again in prison at the war's end. Released, Nakai helped organize a people's university in multiple locations in Hiroshima prefecture that brought together intellectuals, farmers, and laborers, both men and women, and emphasized political self-awareness. He had developed sophisticated

Figure 10.2. Kanamori Tokujiro at the National Diet Library, 1948. Kanamori, center, examines books donated by SCAP. On the right are Nakai Masakazu and Don Brown.

ideas about the evolving role of media in society and is remembered now mainly for this theorizing about film as a medium. He had been director of a small city public library and had a farsighted vision of the potential role of library services in social and political development. He wrote:

> The concept of 'a library without a reading room' is not a paradox; simply by establishing a system of indexing, catalog cards, and a communication network, we shall have a library of vastly different proportions that will offer new kinds of accessibility and service. Even now . . . the library is undergoing a metamorphosis into its future form—from a repository of books to an immense organization redefined as an information center. . . . As print publications are absorbed into microfilm, microfiche, and telephone networks, the concept of the library as a distinct space is destroyed.[13]

Objections to Nakai's left-leaning political views resulted in opposition to his candidacy and led to the appointment of Kanamori, a senior politician and an experienced bureaucrat, as director. Despite protests by conservative librarians, Nakai was appointed vice director, a position created especially for him. This enabled him to focus vigorously on the design and implementation of the Diet Library's policies and practices until he died four years later.

Much needed to be done to develop the operations of this library with its dual roles. To help get the new organization started Robert Downs, a protégé of Charles Harvey Brown, arrived on July 7, 1948, for two months to make more detailed recommendations concerning the new library's operations.

ROBERT DOWNS

Robert Bingham Downs (1903–1991) was tall, gaunt, forceful, autocratic, and diligent. He had been appointed university librarian at the University of Illinois, Urbana–Champaign in 1943, recommended by Charles Harvey Brown. He was also director of the graduate school of librarianship and had served as president of the Association for College and Research Libraries.[14]

During most of the twentieth century, it was common practice to hire a specialized consultant to survey the operations and/or collections of a university library and to make recommendations. Downs was a leading library surveyor, and so he was well prepared for this assignment. Later, by the 1970s, with changes in labor practices, new technology, and a greater emphasis on consultation, such surveys were increasingly performed by committees with diverse membership rather than by an imported surveyor.

Downs was primarily concerned with problems of internal administration and organization, especially the technical procedures for acquiring and processing materials for the library. But he also addressed a wide range of other issues including personnel and the new library's relationship with other libraries. He wrote:

> One point should be emphasized. Every effort has been made to build upon what has already been accomplished by Japanese librarians, rather than try to impose unfamiliar American methods. The Japanese have for a long time shown an active interest in the technical phases of librarianship, and their contributions in this field are significant, especially for Oriental literature. Accordingly, whenever possible, it has been recommended that the National Diet Library adopt procedures already known to Japanese librarians, revising and expanding these methods if necessary or desirable.[15]

Downs also lectured at a summer course in librarianship at the University of Tokyo Library, and Paul Burnette organized a training course at the National Diet Library in the fall of 1948.

Naomi Fukuda, a Japanese librarian trained at the University of Michigan, played a key role as guide and translator. Downs returned to the United States in September 15, 1948, and, having noted the food shortages, sent back food packages.[16]

Housed temporarily in the Akasaka Detached Palace, the National Diet Library was formally inaugurated on June 5 and started providing service the

Figure 10.3. National Diet Library leaders with Naomi Fukuda and Robert Downs.

next day.[17] In the meanwhile, negotiations for legislation for a new law promoting and regulating public libraries as proposed by Philip Keeney had been continuing.

NOTES

1. Charles B. Fahs, *Government in Japan; Recent Trends in Its Scope and Operation* (New York: International Secretariat, Institute of Pacific Relations, 1940). For Fahs and other American experts on Japan, see Richard H. Minear, "Cross-Cultural Perception and World War II: American Japanists of the 1940s and Their Images of Japan," *International Studies Quarterly* 24, no. 4 (December 1980), 555–80.

2. This account is based on U.S. Library Mission to Japan and Supreme Commander for the Allied Powers, Civil Information and Education section, *Report of the United States Library Mission to Advise on the Establishment of the National Diet Library of Japan* (Washington, DC: Government Printing Office, 1948), http://catalog.hathitrust.org/Record/009161030.

3. Verner W. Clapp, "Mission to Japan," *Information Bulletin. Library of Congress* (February 24–March 1, 1948): 7–8, https://catalog.hathitrust.org/Record/000639207.

4. For Clapp, see Foster Mohrhardt, "Clapp, Verner Warren (1901–1972)," 77–81, in *Dictionary of American Library Biography*, edited by Bohdan S. Wynar (Littleton, CO: Libraries Unlimited, 1978); *Verner Warren Clapp, 1901–1972: A Memorial Tribute* (Washington, DC: Library of Congress, 1973).

5. Charles H. Brown, *Scientific Serials* (Chicago: Association of College and Reference Libraries, 1956).

6. For C. H. Brown, see Lawrence S. Thompson, "Brown, Charles Harvey (1875–1960)," 63–65, in *Dictionary of American Library Biography*, edited by Bohdan S. Wynar (Littleton,

CO: Libraries Unlimited, 1978); also, Emily M. Danton, *Pioneering Leaders in Librarianship*, 1st ser. (Chicago: American Library Association, 1953), 293–384; Edward G. Holley, "Charles Harvey Brown," 10–48, in *Leaders in American Academic Librarianship, 1925–1975*, edited by Wayne A. Wiegand (Pittsburgh, PA: Beta Phi Mu; and Chicago: American Library Association, 1983); and Edward G. Holley, "Mr. ACRL: Charles Harvey Brown (1875–1960)," *Journal of Academic Librarianship* 7, no. 5 (November 1981): 271–78.

7. Clapp, "Mission to Japan," 7.
8. U.S. Library Mission, *Report*, 4.
9. U.S. Library Mission, *Report*, 5.
10. U.S. Library Mission, *Report*, 28.
11. U.S. Library Mission, *Report*, 3.

12. For Kanamori, see Justin Williams, *Japan's Political Revolution under MacArthur* (Athens: University of Georgia Press, 1979), 193, 231–44; Clapp, "Mission to Japan," 8; Robert L. Gitler, *Robert Gitler and the Japan Library School* (Lanham, MD: Scarecrow Press, 1999), 92–94; and Haruyama Meitetsu, "Kanamori Tokujiro to sousouki no Kokuritsu Kokkai Toshokan : sengo Nihon niokeru aru 'toshokangaku' no tanjo" [Kanamori Tokujiro and the Early National Diet Library: The Birth of Some 'Librarianship' in Postwar Japan], in Madoko Kon and Masaya Takayama, *Gendai Nihon no toshokan kōsō: sengo kaikaku to sono tenkai* (Tokyo: Bensei Shuppan, 2013), 39–85.

13. For Nakai, see Michael Lucken, *Nakai Masakazu: Naissance de la théorie critique au Japon* (Dijon: Les presses du réel, 2016), esp. 205–18 on the Diet Library; also, Leslie Pincus, "Revolution in the Archives of Memory: The Founding of the National Diet Library in Occupied Japan," 382–92, in *Archives, Documentation, and Institutions of Social Memory: Essays from the Sawyer Seminar*, edited by Francis X. Blouin Jr. and William G. Rosenberg (Ann Arbor: University of Michigan Press, 1981. The quotations are from Pincus (388), who cites Nakai Masakazu, *Nakai Masakazu zenshū*, Kuno Osamu hen (Tokyo: Bijutsu Shuppansha, 1981), 4: 295. "Masakazu Nakai," *Wikipedia*, https://en.wikipedia.org/wiki/Masakazu_Nakai.

14. For Downs, see D. W. Krummel, "Downs, Robert Bingham (1903–1991)," 79–82, in *Dictionary of American Library Biography: Second Supplement*, edited by D. G. Davis (Westport, CT: Libraries Unlimited, 2003); and *Research Librarianship: Essays in Honor of Robert B. Downs*, edited by Jerrold Orne (New York: Bowker, 1971).

15. Robert B. Downs, *National Diet Library. Report on Technical Processes, Bibliographical Services and General Organization* (Tokyo: National Diet Library, 1948). Summary in Verner W. Clapp, "R. B. Downs Reports on the National Diet Library of Japan," *Library of Congress Information Bulletin* (September 21–27, 1948): 17, https://catalog.hathitrust.org/Record/000639207.

16. Clapp, "R. B. Downs," 17.

17. "Japan's 'Library of Congress,'" *Library of Congress. Information Bulletin* (July 27–August 2, 1948): 11–13, https://catalog.hathitrust.org/Record/000639207.

Chapter Eleven

The Library Law of 1950

It was said that substance had been sacrificed for shadow. —Takeuchi Satoru, 1983

The library visions of the education mission, of Keeney's plan, and of Japanese library leaders were ambitious, but their aspirations were not new. The levels of development of library services in Europe and North America were known in Japan. In 1938, for example, the All-Japan Library Conference had petitioned the Education Council of the Ministry of Education to mandate public libraries throughout the country with massive funding from the central government.[1] But government interest in supporting public libraries remained minimal.[2]

Successive Japanese governments sought to adopt and adapt the best of Western science and technology, and they paid serious attention to scientific and technology literature. Libraries "leak," in the sense that new and culturally different ideas come in through books and magazines and are disseminated through library readers. Library services that encourage new ideas and independent thinking do not suit authoritarian regimes, conformist societies, or wherever educational instruction is didactic and aligned with examinations. And where libraries provide little service, the librarians' need for professional education is limited to training in technical procedures. For whatever reasons, in Japan the government had been content with a rather minimal level of investment in public libraries and in education for librarians.

Military defeat and the occupation in 1945 made the advancement of democracy a high official priority, and that implied wider access to information. Establishment of the National Diet Library represented a major change and was symbolic of a new and different regime, but the development of public libraries remained undecided. Not all democracies are liberal. Countries with "democratic" in their official name often have been illiberal, repressive regimes. Western liberal democracy is associated with an informed, educated citizenry in the United States, where by 1945 the need for free public library services had long been generally accepted. Further, public libraries were at that time seen as playing a major role in adult education, as "the people's university." This view was reflected in the education mission's recommendations for the development of library services as shown in chapter 8.

NAKATA'S DRAFT

The education mission's report had been submitted on March 30, 1946, and Keeney's plan a few days later. Any significant change to library services would require legislation, so the Ministry of Education asked Nakata Kunizo to draft a new library law taking into account prior Japanese experience and opinions. Nakata worked with others on a draft plan that was submitted in June 1946.

Nakata's plan proposed a network of various types of libraries, a national central library and prefectural central libraries to serve as centers for the network, legislation requiring each local government to provide local public libraries, and liaison bureaus and liaison officers at the central and prefectural central libraries. The plan can be viewed as a natural extension of long-held aspirations of leading Japanese library leaders, but now enhanced by the SCAP initiatives.[3] Nakata and his collaborators included substantial requirements and provisions for the education of librarians because they knew that education for librarianship would not be developed otherwise. The plan included a central, national library school to prepare librarians for large libraries and many smaller library schools for training staff for small libraries.

At the conference of August 15–18, 1946, called by the Ministry of Education to discuss the draft legislation and at which Keeney had hosted a dinner, the following issues were discussed at length:[4]

- The necessity of financial help from the national government for the rehabilitation of bombed libraries. Seventeen prefectural libraries had been wholly or partially destroyed.
- Support for buying expensive books.
- Strengthening the Ueno Imperial Library so that it would play a part in Japanese life comparable to that played by the Library of Congress.
- The immediate establishment of an adequate library school. All librarians considered the lack of trained librarians one of the most serious drawbacks to the progress of Japanese librarianship. Ministry officials agreed to give this their immediate attention.

- A strong prefectural library was to be erected in each prefecture with help for all new construction from the national government.
- The desirability of establishing a library bureau in the ministry to conform with the recommendation proposed by the U.S. education mission. This subject received a great deal of serious attention on the part of the delegates.
- Improved tenure, promotion, and salaries for librarians, "among the poorest paid professionals in Japan."

JOHN NELSON

When Philip Keeney was removed from his position in April 1947, his duties were assigned to John Nelson, who worked with Kato Shukoh on a sixth version of the ministry's library plan. Nelson urged that the plan be expressed legislatively as a library law.

John Monninger Nelson was the CIE education division's adult education officer from 1946 to 1950. Like his division head, Mark T. Orr, Nelson used his CIE experience as the basis for a doctoral dissertation on adult education in Japan after his return to the United States. It includes an account of visiting a grim and unfriendly public library where he was offended by the use of wire mesh to protect the library's books from readers, who could see but not touch what was on the shelves.[5] Nelson was a young educator from Kansas, not an experienced librarian. He would not have known that this use of wire mesh had been standard practice in American public libraries, or that the standard manual on public library services of the previous generation, Arthur Bostwick's *Administration of a Public Library*, contained illustrations of the same use of wire mesh in branches of the New York Public Library.[6]

The position of library officer had been created within the CIE education division for Philip Keeney and later was held by Paul Burnette. However, responsibility within SCAP for providing advice and assistance concerning libraries was, in practice, divided between several occupation officials. Occupation personnel concerned with higher education provided advice regarding university and college libraries. Personnel concerned with elementary and secondary schools worked with Japanese personnel in improving school libraries. SCAP's government section and CIE had cooperated in securing the services of Verner W. Clapp and Charles H. Brown at the request of the Japanese Diet to advise the Japanese government regarding the National Diet Library. The CIE information centers were supervised by personnel of the information division of CIE, under Don Brown, not the education division, which housed the library officer. The audiovisual officer in the education division was responsible for supervising the establishment and operation of an audiovisual library in each prefectural library. John Nelson, as adult education specialist, was concerned with public libraries as they could be used to support adult education.

In October 1947 Paul Burnette was designated library officer. He resigned in March 1949 and was replaced in April 1949 by Jane Fairweather, who had been chief army librarian for the Far East Command, also based at general headquarters in Tokyo. But she returned to the United States in September 1949. With Burnette's departure Nelson again assumed responsibility within CIE for library matters, including working with officials in the bureau of social education within the Japanese Ministry of Education and representatives of the Japanese Library Association in drafting a new public library law. Keeney and Burnette appear to have built good relationships with Japanese librarians, and a better outcome might have resulted had either been in the position throughout. The instability in the position of CIE library officer was unfortunate, and Nelson had the disadvantage of not being a librarian.

After endless discussions, a sixteenth draft law mandated public libraries in every local government jurisdiction, with more than ten thousand libraries, mostly very small, projected with thirty-six thousand full-time library employees. The twenty-first draft, now in a period of greater financial austerity, no longer mandated the provision of library services and weakened the education requirements for chief librarians. The Japanese library leaders decided to acquiesce to the ministry, and an even weaker twenty-second version was enacted as the Library Law of 1950 and promulgated on April 30, 1950.[7]

THE LIBRARY LAW OF 1950

A significant minority of libraries serving the general public were provided privately, not from public funds, so the law to authorize and regulate public libraries was called the Library Law rather than the Public Library Law.[8]

Statistics from a survey by the ministry's bureau of social education in March 1949 had reported a total of 1,549 public libraries with, on average, about 5,300 Japanese books and 400 Western books. Because these counts included prefectural libraries, which were relatively large, most libraries had less. Few had more than 3,000 volumes, and most had very low attendance.

The new Library Law was very important because it authorized local government authorities to provide free public library service. It also provided a mechanism and conditions for financial support by the central government to such libraries as met minimum standards to be established by the minister of education, but it did not allocate any funds. The law clarified definitions, responsibilities, and relationships. It mandated cooperation and interlibrary loan between public libraries and the National Diet Library, stipulated that public library services be provided for free, provided for advisory library councils, decentralized responsibility for public library services to the prefectural level or below, associated public library districts with school districts, and mandated professional qualifications for chief librarians and their assistants.[9]

Article 1 declared, "The purpose of this Law is to provide for necessary matters concerning the establishment and operation of libraries, and to promote a sound development thereof, and thereby to contribute to the enhancement of the education and culture of the nation, in accordance with the spirit of the Social Education Law." Libraries were expected to "collect arrange and keep in custody books, archives and other necessary data and materials for the purpose of making them serviceable, by offering them for the utilization of the general public, to their self-education, research and survey, recreation and other purposes" (Article §2). The law's provisions and expectations included:

- An expectation for library service, not merely passive collections: "Efforts shall be made that the library personnel may get adequate knowledge of the library materials and may give counsel to the visitors for their utilization of the library materials" (§2)
- A range of materials: "sufficient attention being paid so that such materials as local materials, art works, materials of local administration, gramophone records and films will also be collected" (§3(1))
- Library outreach: "Branch libraries, reading-centers and book-circulating centers may be established, and the service of bookmobiles and itinerant lending libraries may be offered. Reading-circles, seminars, appreciation meetings, showing of films, exhibitions of data and materials, etc. shall be sponsored and encouraged. Information and reference materials concerning current problems shall be introduced and offered to the general public" (§3(3, 5–7))
- Each library should function as part of a national system: "Close contact and collaboration shall be made between libraries and with the National Diet Library, libraries attached to the assemblies of local public bodies and libraries attached to schools by such means as inter-library loans. . . . Close contact and cooperation shall be made with schools, museums, citizens' public halls, research institutes, etc." (§3(4 & 8))
- Every library must have a professionally qualified chief library: Assistant librarians must also be professionally qualified. Since most librarians did not have currently have formal professional qualifications, a five-year transition period was allowed. (§13)
- Service must be free: "Public libraries shall not charge any admission fee nor any other compensation for use of the library materials." (§17)
- Standards: "The Minister of Education shall in order to promote the sound development of libraries formulate desirable standards for the establish-

ment and the operation of public libraries and make them available to the Boards of Education for guidance and in addition, make them known to the general public." (§19)
- Authorized financial support by the central government for libraries that met the standards: "The State shall within the limits of budgetary appropriations, grant promotional subsidies for the expenses required for the establishment and the operation of the libraries and other types of necessary assistance to the local public bodies that establish the libraries." (§20)

A SHADOW

With the implementation of the Library Law's requirements, many existing small libraries closed, and only 12 percent of cities, towns, and villages had libraries. Nevertheless, the new Library Law required an estimated fifteen hundred librarians to obtain a minimal professional qualification and another estimated fifteen hundred assistant librarians to obtain a comparable qualification within the next five years. In fact, the Ueno Park Librarian Training Institute, administered by the Ministry of Education, had been revived in 1947 with a two-year program. Completion of this course would qualify, but it remained small, graduating only twelve students in 1950. The newly imposed requirement would have to be met by new programs at other institutions. The law specified as a minimal threshold an introductory program of fifteen credits covering basic library procedures that in the United States would have been regarded as suitable for a library assistant. Providing such a basic course was not difficult if an experienced librarian or two could be found to teach it. Several universities soon began to offer programs meeting the new law's modest requirement.

These provisions more or less match Gillis's California county library system, with two significant differences. The Library Law placed libraries under local boards of education whereas Gillis had kept county library services in California administratively separate from county boards of education. Also, the California county library system emphasized large service units: the entire county excluding incorporated cities that chose to provide library services separately. Large service units providing local branches can afford specialized experts and provide a much more advanced range of services than multiple small, separate service units ever could.

The relationship between Keeney's plan and the new law is unclear because of the complexity of the discussions and revisions leading up to enactment of the law, because ideas adopted in the law had antecedents in Japanese discussions independent of Keeney's plan, and because its features could have been expected, more or less, in any national public library plan at that time.

Unfortunately, although the Library Law authorized a free public library system for Japan, public service and interinstitutional collaboration were specified, and professional education was mandated, the new law was not accompanied by implementation at the level hoped for. After some twenty revisions, the ministry had removed the strongest elements, leaving a much-diluted program. Takeuchi Satoru commented, "It was said that substance had been sacrificed for shadow."[10]

Authorizing and providing mechanisms for funding from the central government constituted an important preparatory step, but would have little effect if funding were not allocated. Funding remained meager.

Professional training had become mandatory, another important step, but the level was set far below what Carnovsky, Keeney, or Burnette would have considered needed. The Library Law of 1950 remained in effect for more than fifty years. The low threshold to qualify formally as a chief librarian (*shisho*) or assistant librarian (*shishoho*) facilitated the acceptance of requiring professional education, but a low qualification requirement does not bring much status or claim to a good salary. Also, a minimal requirement is likely to remove the incentive to obtain more substantial professional qualifications when they became available. In fact, the courses for librarians became extremely popular among students, far in excess of any imaginable employment in libraries. So, although the new law authorized progress toward a unified library system for Japan, public library services and the professional preparation for librarianship were to remain weak. In Japanese local government administration, it has been considered good management practice to rotate staff around different departments, so librarians, not being regarded as a separate profession, were liable to be reassigned to some other city department, such as accounting or human resources. This doubtless has some benefits, but it inhibited professional identity as librarians.

Looking back at the period from 1946 to 1950, Nelson concluded that improvement of public libraries "cannot be listed as a major accomplishment, except for their expansion of audio-visual educational activities. . . . Providing adequate library buildings and equipment and raising the standards of library services in Japan was greatly handicapped by lack of funds."[11] Nevertheless, the law did provide for free public library service, recognition of professional library staff, and mandated professional education.

Around the same time that the Library Law was passed, in the spring of 1950, SCAP's civil information and education section witnessed a surprising development.

NOTES

1. Theodore F. Welch, *Libraries and Librarianship in Japan* (Westport: Greenwood, 1997), 74–75.

2. This chapter follows the detailed account in Takeuchi Satoru, "Education for Librarianship in Japan: A Comparative Study of the Pre-1945 and Post-1945 Periods" (PhD diss., University of Pittsburgh, 1979), chap. 5: The Library Law and Education for Librarianship (1946–1955). Note also Takeuchi Satoru, "Japan, Education for Library and Information Science," 239–71, in *Encyclopedia of Library and Information Science*, vol. 36 (New York: Marcel Dekker, 1983); and *Toshokanhō seiritsushi shiryō*, edited by Urata Takeo and Ogawa Takeshi (Tokyo: Nihon Toshokan Kyōkai, 1968). See also Miura Taro, "Senryouka Nihon niokeru toshokanhou seitei katei" [The Enactment Process of the Library Law during Occupation in Japan], in Madoko Kon and Masaya Takayama, *Gendai Nihon no toshokan kōsō: sengo kaikaku to sono tenkai* (Tokyo: Bensei Shuppan, 2013, 249–70.

3. Takeuchi, "Education," 134.

4. Keeney to Orr, memorandum, September 1, 1946. Reprinted in Urata and Ogawa, *Toshokanhō*, 438–41. Copy in Keeney Papers, box 2: 1.

5. John M. Nelson, "The Adult-Education Program in Occupied Japan, 1946–1950" (PhD diss., University of Kansas, 1954). Japanese translation *Senryōki Nihon no shakai kyōiku kaikaku* (Tokyo: Ōzorasha, 1990).

6. Arthur E. Bostwick, *The American Public Library*, 3rd ed. (New York: Appleton, 1928).

7. An English text of the law is in appendix 2 in Theodore F. Welch, *Toshokan: Libraries in Japanese Society* (London: Bingley, 1976), 253–60; also in Nelson, "The Adult-Education," 418–37. Welch's text lists articles 7, 11, 22, and 24 as "deleted" and provides no text. Nelson provides the text of these articles, makes no mention of deletion, and may be an earlier version.

8. Nelson, "The Adult-Education," 448–49. For details of the law, see Urata and Ogawa, *Toshokanhō*.

9. Welch, *Toshokan*, 57–60, 253–60; Welch, *Libraries*, 74–75.

10. Takeuchi, "Japan," 248.

11. Nelson, "The Adult-Education," 354–55.

Chapter Twelve

Don Brown's Initiative

And in a flash I said, "Why don't we start a library training institute?" —Don Brown, 1976

DONALD NUGENT

The head of the Civil Information and Education section (CIE) of SCAP for most of the Occupation period was a Marine Corps lieutenant colonel named Donald Nugent. He had joined the education division of CIE in February 1946 and quickly became its head and then chief of CIE for the rest of the Occupation.

Donald Ross Nugent (1903–1983) was born in San Jose, California, and attended Stanford University, where he received a BA in history and a master's degree in education. He taught at a community college and compiled (and largely wrote) an impressive students' guide to Asian studies, *The Pacific Area and Its Problems; A Study Guide*. He had had prewar experience of Japan, including teaching for some years in Wakayama. Although he preferred to use English, he could converse in Japanese.[1]

Early in 1950, Nugent summoned Don Brown, head of CIE's information division, to his office to join a discussion with a visitor, Lou Van Wagoner. A former field artillery officer, Van Wagoner was visiting from Washington, DC, where he worked for the Government Account for Relief in Occupied Areas (GARIOA). Van Wagoner's duties included procuring materials and services that CIE needed. He explained to Nugent and Brown that CIE had a significant unspent funding balance that would be lost to CIE and reassigned elsewhere unless spent or at least committed to a specific future expense before the end of the federal fiscal year, which at that time ended on June 30.

When Van Wagoner asked whether CIE had a good use for this money, Don Brown immediately proposed using it to educate librarians. He later recalled,

> And in a flash I said, "Why don't we start a library training institute?" I was fully familiar with such libraries as Ueno, Hibiya Public Library, Library at Todai, Toyo Bunko Library and the Kokusai Bunka Shinkokai Library. . . . I might add that I have been using libraries since the age of six. I am very familiar with libraries from the consumers' viewpoints.[2]

Nugent agreed and asked Van Wagoner to help make that happen. Nugent has been described as an unimaginative, stodgy administrator, but, as Brown later emphasized, the suggestion to use the money to train librarians would have gone nowhere if Nugent had not fully supported the idea.[3]

Small steps had been taken to resume education for librarians after the war. The Ueno Library Training School resumed in 1947 with an expanded two-year program and now required junior college education for admission. A program existed briefly at Kyoto University in 1948. CIE itself conducted a series of popular training programs known as Institutes for Educational Leadership (IFEL) starting in 1948. These were intensive refresher courses in twenty-five different professional and technical areas, and four IFEL institutes were for librarians. The first two were offered in 1949 by Jane Fairweather, a U.S. Army librarian then working for CIE. Two more were held in 1950 and 1951, taught by Susan Grey Akers, dean of the library school at the University of North Carolina. Although the IFEL institutes were highly regarded, the number of participants in these programs was much too small to make much difference.[4]

THE AMERICAN LIBRARY ASSOCIATION

After Van Wagoner had returned to Washington, the army contacted Verner Clapp, the deputy librarian of Congress, who had chaired the mission with Charles Harvey Brown that made recommendations concerning the new National Diet Library.[5] On May 19, 1950, an internal memo at American Library Association's headquarters summarized a telephone message from Verner Clapp to John Cory, who had succeeded Carl Milam as ALA's executive director. John Mackenzie Cory was a Berkeley-trained librarian whose varied career included being chief of the library division of the Office of Wartime Information advising OWI on library needs and facilities and assisting libraries in planning war information programs.[6]

> Mr. Clapp said for the last year and a half he has been talking with the Army and Occupation authorities to get Japanese librarians to come to this country.

> Suddenly the Army has called him to tell him that the Army now has funds for $100,000 for library education. . . . This $100,000 is to be spent for the establishment of a library school or a library institution for teaching librarianship in Japan. This must go into operation by April 1, 1951.
> The telegram Col. Hodges received regarding this measure advised that Columbia University be contacted. Mr. Clapp suggested that rather than doing that, the Army make a contract with ALA to do the job, with ALA assuming full responsibility for staff, personnel, etc.[7]

The American Library Association (ALA) had a well-established interest in the development of library services outside the United States. An International Relations Board had been established in 1942 and funded from 1943 by the Rockefeller Foundation. ALA officials, notably the long-serving executive secretary, Carl Milam, had been actively engaged in the development of U.S.-funded libraries in Latin America. More significantly, ALA had sponsored establishment of a successful school for librarians in Paris, France, which had operated from 1924 to 1929 and had had a significant influence on the turmoil of professional library developments in France between the two world wars.[8] In 1943 Edwin E. Williams had prepared a report for ALA's International Relations Board on needs and opportunities for library development after the war. He wrote concerning Japan:

> Japan, it may be added, is an even more difficult problem than the enemy countries in Europe. The internal results of defeat can hardly be guessed in an Oriental nation that has never known defeat and has had no experience with a liberal government. Possibly the Chinese or the Koreans, who appear to be less vindictive than many of the European victims of aggression, may be better fitted than any western nation for the task of bringing Japan back into a system of world intellectual intercourse. In any case, war should not blind Japan's opponents to the fact that the Japanese are capable of making and have made, useful contributions to world scholarship and culture. Japanese librarians can profit from training in this country.[9]

A 1947 policy document of ALA's International Relations Board stated:

> The International relations Board of the American Library Association believes that librarians, libraries and the materials with which they work are vital to the establishment and assurance of a lasting peace. . . . Now that the hostilities are over, it seems inconceivable that the American Library Association should limit its activities to national issues and not seek means to promote international understanding.[10]

In 1949 the Rockefeller Foundation had granted ALA $7,000 to purchase materials on library science for the University of Tokyo. Basic materials and materials were sent during 1949 and 1950 "to stimulate the work of those already in the field in Japan."

The army's offer relayed by Verner Clapp was accepted, and the International Relations Board, chaired by Flora Belle Ludington, established an advisory committee for the Japanese Library School Project, chaired by Robert Downs. Ludington had been librarian at Mills College, near Berkeley, and then was for many years the librarian of Mount Holyoke College in Massachusetts. On leave from Mount Holyoke, she had been founding director of the U.S. information library in Bombay from 1944 to 1946 and a visiting expert at CIE in Japan in 1948.[11]

The executive board of ALA voted to delegate to the International Relations Board full power to act as necessary in the establishment of a library school in Japan, and ALA submitted a formal proposal for army approval on August 25, 1950. A diverse advisory committee for the project was created that included Verner Clapp, Mae Graham, and Robert Downs as chair. Paul Burnette, a member of the International Relations Board and at that time working for Downs at the University of Illinois, Urbana–Champaign, was given three months' leave of absence to assemble materials for the new school. Downs published an article about the project:

> The curriculum of the [Japan] library school is being planned to meet the needs of the following groups: (1) beginning students; (2) in-service librarians who must meet the requirements of the library law; (3) teachers of librarianship. Although the school will be able to accommodate only 50 to 100 students, it is felt that the teachers of librarianship who receive their training there can in turn assist in training beginning students and the great number of in-service librarians. The library school will emphasize the practice rather than the theory of librarianship, and will attempt to imbue its students with an understanding of the worth and opportunity for service of libraries and librarians in Japan. . . . After a period of 15 months, continuation of the school will be the responsibility of the sponsoring university.[12]

THE ARMY'S COMMITMENT

R. P. Hagen, acting chief of the reorientation branch of the army's Office for Occupied Areas, wrote to Flora Belle Ludington on October 12, 1950:

> Since it is proposed that the American staff be employed as Department of the Army consultants, SCAP feels that the school should be described as a SCAP project, administered by the Department of the Army consultants, chosen, supervised and assisted, under contract, by the American Library Association. SCAP expresses a strong hope that the school, its faculty and curriculum, will recognize the great need for young men and women so imbued with conviction of the importance of libraries as tools for use by the people in pursuit of the democratic goal of realizing their fullest potentialities that, equipped with the fundamentals of the organization, administration, promotion and utilization of libraries, they would yield to no opposition or discouragement, persuade com-

munities without libraries to establish libraries, no matter how small, and stimulate libraries into greater public service. It is suggested that the school place first emphasis on creating an attitude toward librarianship and library service of such intensity that its graduates would be not only immune to the conservative passivity of the existing Japanese library profession but also be able to galvanize or enflame the profession into activity. It is felt that the curriculum should include courses in book selection and classification, together with training in how to make the materials in the library most easily accessible to those desiring to use them, in lending methods, and in the preparation of bibliographies. But there should also be courses on how to finance a small library, how to win community support, how to attract people into the library, and all aspects of making the library useful.[13]

DOWNS'S SURVEY

In the meanwhile, the International Relations Committee had arranged for Robert Downs to conduct a preliminary survey of universities in Japan that might be suitable locations for a school of librarianship. He was the director of the library school, as well as university librarian, at the University of Illinois, Urbana–Champaign, and he had recent experience in Japan when advising the National Diet Library. Downs went to Japan and, again aided by Naomi Fukuda, consulted widely. He was eager for the project to succeed. He wrote later in his autobiography, "The most serious weakness of librarianship in Japan at the time was the scarcity of librarians and the lack of training agencies."[14]

Downs reported that he believed the project to start a college-level school of librarianship was both desirable and feasible. He identified and commented on some universities as potential hosts: The University of Tokyo, Kyoto University, Doshisha, Keio, and Waseda. A thirty-eight-page final report dated July 17, 1950, was submitted to the ALA International Relations Committee, and a summary dated August 25 was sent to the army.

APPOINTING A DIRECTOR

The selection committee developed a short list of three candidates. One was Louis Shores (1904–1981), then part-time director of the library school at Florida State University and part-time encyclopedia editor. Shores is remembered for emphasizing the central educational role of libraries and using the phrase "library college" rather than "college library." Another was Jerrold Orne (1911–2008), then library director at Washington University in St. Louis, who had had experience at the Library of Congress and with the handling of technical literature. The third short-listed candidate, whose name had been suggested by Paul Burnette, was Robert Gitler, then director of the

University of Washington library school in Seattle, who was approached late in the summer of 1950. Leon Carnovsky had been approached but declined.

Time appears to have been lost because the ALA was not assured that the funding was definite until well into October. SCAP wanted the opportunity to comment on the candidates being considered before a final decision was made and imposed the significant limitation that no spouse or other dependent would be allowed to accompany the appointee because of the increasingly dangerous situation in nearby Korea. However, the army considered these short-listed candidates to be acceptable. A small advisory committee, chaired by Robert Downs and including Verner Clapp, was created to advise the school and its director.

In mid-October Ludington contacted Gitler, who responded positively. The University of Washington was willing to grant him a year of leave without pay. He was offered the assignment, and he accepted. Flora Belle Ludington informed Nugent on November 8, 1950, that Robert Gitler had been selected. The next step was for Gitler to go to Japan.

NOTES

1. *The Pacific Area and Its Problems: A Study Guide*, edited by Donald R. Nugent (New York: American Council, Institute of Pacific Relations, 1936). Don Brown, *Beginning of the School*, unedited transcript of talk given November 28, 1976; Robert S. Schwantes, *Japanese and Americans: A Century of Cultural Relations* (New York: Harper, 1955), 127.

2. Brown, *Beginning*, 3.

3. Theodore Cohen, *Remaking Japan: The American Occupation as New Deal* (New York: Free Press, 1987), 97.

4. Takahisa Sawamoto, "Training and Education Programs for Librarians in Japan," 65–72, in *Library Education in Developing Countries*, edited by George S. Bonn ([Honolulu: East-West Center Press, 1966). Also Takeuchi Satoru, "Education for Librarianship in Japan: A Comparative Study of the Pre-1945 and Post-1945 Periods" (PhD diss., University of Pittsburgh, 1979), chap. 5: The Library Law and Education for Librarianship (1946–1955); Takeuchi Satoru, "Japan, Education for Library and Information Science," 239–71, in *Encyclopedia of Library and Information Science*, 36 (New York: Marcel Dekker, 1983); Suzuki Yukihisa, "American Influence on the Development of Library Services in Japan 1860–1948" (PhD diss., University of Michigan, 1974); Beverly J. Brewster, *American Overseas Library Technical Assistance, 1940–1970* (Metuchen, NJ: Scarecrow Press, 1976), 87, n. 54; and Robert L. Gitler, "Japan," *Library Trends* 12, no. 2 (October 1963): 273–94.

5. Downs stated that MacArthur himself proposed the project to Clapp and Downs at a luncheon at the Library of Congress. *Oriental Collections, U.S.A. and Abroad. Report of the Third Group Meeting Held at the University of Pennsylvania, March 28, 1951*. Sponsored by the Joint Committee of the Far Eastern Association and the American Library Association (Ames: Office of the Chairman, Iowa State College Library, 1951), 3.

6. For Cory, see Peggy Sulllivan, "Cory, John Mackenzie (1914–1988)," 55–58, in *Dictionary of American Library Biography: Second Supplement*, edited by Donald G. Davis (Westport, CT: Libraries Unlimited, 2003).

7. Margie Sornson Malmberg to Cory, memo, May 19, 1950. ALA Archives. Executive Board and Executive Director. Subject File, 1910–1976. Series 2/4/6. Box 22.

8. S. W. Witt, "Merchants of Light: The Paris Library School, Internationalism, and the Globalization of a Profession," *Library Quarterly* 83, no. 2 (April 2013): 1–21.

9. Edwin Everitt Williams, *International Library Relations: A General Survey of Possible Postwar Library Development* (Chicago: American Library Association, 1943), 7.

10. American Library Association, "Conclusions and Recommendations of the International Relations Board." Memorandum (March 26, 1947), 1–2.

11. Anne C. Edmonds, "Ludington, Flora Belle (1898–1967)," 322–24, in *Dictionary of American Library Biography*, edited by Bohdan S. Wynar (Westport, CT: Libraries Unlimited, 1978).

12. "Japanese Library School," *ALA Bulletin* 44 (December 1950): 458; Robert B. Downs, "ALA Sponsorship of Library Schools Abroad: How to Start a Library School," *ALA Bulletin*, 52 (June 1958): 388–400.

13. Hagen to Ludington, October 12, 1950. ALA.

14. Robert B. Downs, *Perspectives on the Past: An Autobiography* (Metuchen, NJ: Scarecrow Press, 1984), 122.

Chapter Thirteen

Gitler, Kiyooka, and Keio

I think I must have felt like Brigham Young felt when he reached the Great Salt Lake and said, "This is the place!" —Robert Gitler, 1999

ROBERT GITLER

Robert Gitler's career is described at length in his autobiography, an edited version of reminiscences recorded in his old age.[1] He was born in 1909 in New York City and taken to San Francisco around 1912 after his mother's arranged marriage to a much older Russian immigrant ended in divorce. He grew up in Oakland, which then had excellent public schools, and attended the nearby University of California in Berkeley. Gitler enjoyed performing in amateur dramatics and worked as a student assistant in the university library. Graduating in May 1930 with a BA in history and political science, he fancied a career in the foreign service, but he missed the exams through illness, and appendicitis prevented a planned trip to Spain. The Great Depression had started, and he had no money, no prospects, and no plans. Sydney Mitchell, director of Berkeley's school of librarianship, who had influenced Philip Keeney, suggested to Gitler that he consider qualifying as a librarian. Gitler believed that libraries were both interesting and beneficial, and he entered Berkeley's one-year graduate certificate program, which was essentially the same as when Keeney had been there a decade earlier.

Robert Gitler had a positive attitude to life and its possibilities. In his final years, he had a plaque on his wall with the inscription that he regarded as his philosophy: "Do not follow where the path may lead. Go instead where there is no path, and leave a trail." He needed a positive attitude in 1950 because he faced a very large challenge. He was expected to open a new school of librarianship in Japan when the Japanese academic year began at the beginning of April, just months away, and as yet no university had agreed to host the planned school. Japanese universities were notably traditional and conservative. He was to start a college-level program in a field not regarded as a college-level subject, and he had to persuade the host university to assume full future financial responsibility when his temporary funding expired. He knew no Japanese and little about Japan. It was a mission that seemed unlikely to succeed.

Gitler met with the American Library Association advisory committee in November and soon reported to Flora Belle Ludington, chair of ALA's International Relations Board, that "I had a most satisfactory conference Saturday [December 2, 1950] in the Pentagon with Col. Van Wagoner and Lt. Col. Nugent."[2]

He finally reached Tokyo on December 22 and reported the next day to the CIE headquarters, where he met Don Brown. Because it was Christmas, Brown took Gitler with him to a gathering of the information center librarians at Kawana, a large resort hotel overlooking the sea. He found these American librarians very supportive and helpful, even willing to recommend their own best advisers as possible translators to staff the new school.

Promptly on his return from Kawana, Gitler paid a courtesy call on Dr. Amano at the Ministry of Education and on Dr. Kanamori, the National Diet librarian, whom he had met previously at an ALA conference. Many years later Gitler recollected the meeting:

> Don Brown told me, "I think you will find Miss Fukuda is there, Naomi Fukuda. She is a very remarkable lady." She was a major figure in so many things in postwar Japan and a remarkable human being. Miss Ludington had told me about her before I got to Japan.... At the far end of the room, on a dais, sat Dr. Kanamori on a throne-like chair, ... At his left shoulder, there was Miss Fukuda. She was doing the interpreting for him.... I had a delightful visit with Dr. Kanamori. He was very aware of what was going on by way of the library education program, and of libraries in general.[3]

WHICH UNIVERSITY?

Gitler visited the five universities that Robert Downs had identified and narrowed the options to three: Keio, Kyoto National, and Tokyo. One difficulty, especially at the University of Tokyo, was that although campus administrators were willing to accept extramural funding to creating a temporary institute, they were unwilling to have what Gitler wanted: a regular academic department with a campus commitment to assume permanent funding.[4] In a conscientious effort to be objective, he made a list of sixteen criteria:

Figure 13.1. Robert Gitler, 1956.

1. General philosophy, understanding, and acceptance of Western concepts, ideas, and approaches to education.
2. Willingness and ability to accept transfer students from other institutions of higher education, allowing credit for work taken elsewhere toward the degree of the institution to which the student had transferred.
3. Interest in and commitment to the continuation of the library school after 1952.
4. Relative tuition costs of universities.
5. Extent to which university's administrative organization allows for delegation of direction of the school and formulating of its policies and programs to the ALA representatives.
6. Acceptance of visiting Japanese faculty of the library school to the university staff.
7. Assistance in processing of admissions, keeping of student records.
8. Willingness to admit "in-service" students for special inter-sessions or summer sessions.
9. Strength of the library's collections of Oriental materials.
10. Strength of the library's collections of Western materials.
11. Strength of the library's collections of materials relating to library science.
12. Availability of scholarship funds.
13. Physical facilities available to the school.
14. Student housing facilities and relative costs.
15. Geographical location, university's prestige as a factor in attracting students.
16. Geographical location as a logistic factor in liaison with CI&E.

Gitler was well aware that some of these criteria were quite subjective and that, where they were quantitative, he did not always have reliable data. Nevertheless, he tried to be scrupulously fair as he rated Keio, Kyoto National, and Tokyo universities on a scale of 1 to 5 for each criterion and tallied the results.

KIYOOKA EIICHI

Gitler visited Keio University on January 10, where he met with Professor Kiyooka Eiichi, head of the international department. Professor Kiyooka explained that it was the birthday of his grandfather, Fukuzawa Yukichi, who had founded Keio in order to import Western learning.

Kiyooka (1902–1997) spoke fluent English. As a young man he had been sent to the United States to train as an engineer in preparation for a role in a family business. But at Cornell University, he had quietly changed to English literature without telling his family. After graduating in 1927, he spent forty days driving west with friends in a model-T Ford, making a film of the trip.[5]

Keio University was part of a family of institutions founded by Fukuzawa; and instead of becoming an engineer, Kiyooka became principal of Keio's primary school. A moderate, deeply liberal in his convictions and with a fondness for English and American literature and culture, Kiyooka found the increasingly authoritarian, militaristic government policies distressing. He did not believe that the emperor was divine, and he felt sure that the bombing of Pearl Harbor would lead to a disastrous military defeat. He did what little he could to avoid or delay the Fascist policies imposed on his school during the war years. The school had to be evacuated from Tokyo for the students' safety, and it was a hard struggle to maintain the school and to feed the students.[6]

Kiyooka had published an English translation of Fukuzawa's autobiography in 1934 and produced a textbook for English-language students to learn Japanese in 1942, *Japanese in Thirty Hours: First Course in Japanese Language*. Both were reissued in several editions over the years. His affinity with U.S. culture was reinforced by his marriage in 1932 to Sugimoto Chiyono, who had been born and educated in the United States.

SUGIMOTO ETSUKO

Kiyooka's mother-in-law, Sugimoto Etsuko (1874–1950, also known as Etsu Inagaki Sugimoto), was born into a provincial samurai family with traditional values. When her brother, the head of the family, learned that one of his friends was now a merchant in Cincinnati, Ohio, and was lonely, he sent his sister to Cincinnati in 1898 to marry his lonely friend. Two daughters were born, then the husband died. Sugimoto returned to Japan, but then went back to the United States with her daughters so that they could complete their education there. She supported herself by teaching Japanese language, culture, and history at Columbia University in New York City.

In 1925 Sugimoto published, in English, an autobiography or, rather, an autobiographical novel, *A Daughter of the Samurai: How a Daughter of Feudal Japan, Living Hundreds of Years in One Generation, Became a Modern American*.[7] The intention was to explain Japanese life to Westerners, especially Americans. It first appeared in installments in a magazine. The book version was secretly rewritten by her friend Florence Wilson; it became a bestseller and was widely assigned reading in U.S. secondary schools. Sugimoto wrote several other books in English, but they were less successful. After the war she welcomed and assisted the occupation administration. "No one was more eager than mother to cooperate with SCAP," wrote her

Figure 13.2. Kiyooka Eiichi and Sugimoto Chiyono.

daughter, Sugimoto Chiyono, in her book about her parents, *But the Ships Are Sailing—Sailing—*, which she wrote to appease readers demanding a sequel to her mother's popular autobiography.[8]

After the war, Kiyooka taught English in Keio University's school of law and was put in charge of an international department, which was intended in part to handle extramural funding. So, he was assigned to meet with Robert Gitler. Having become familiar with library services in the United States, Kiyooka was understandably enthusiastic at the prospect of a U.S.-style school for librarians, and he acted skillfully as the intermediary between Gitler and the "Standing Directors," the university's executive board.

FUKUZAWA AND KEIO

Kiyooka explained to Gitler how the university originated in Fukuzawa's personal mission to introduce Western learning to Japan even before Japan's "opening" in 1853–1854. Fukuzawa was a member of the first Japanese diplomatic mission to the United States, which arrived in San Francisco in

1860. The mission's visit to the Mercantile Library Association library inspired the creation of naval libraries in Japan. Fukuzawa found a Webster's dictionary with which he could begin serious study of the English language. He became an official translator, visited Europe, published numerous books explaining Western ways—including libraries—and brought back many books.[9] Fukuzawa devoted himself to educating his countrymen in new ways of thinking in order to enable Japan to resist European imperialism.

In 1858 Fukuzawa had established a school to teach Dutch, and from then on he devoted his time to education. In 1868 Fukuzawa changed the school's name to Keio Gijuku, where Keio denotes the period (1865–1868) and Gijuku means school. He provided detailed regulations for its library based on European and American practice and added public speaking to the curriculum. Although Keio's initial identity was that of a private school of Western studies, it expanded and established its first university faculty in 1890. Fukuzawa wrote to the president of Harvard University asking him to help him by sending some American professors, and three came. With this ancestry, Keio University is the oldest existing institution of higher learning in Japan.[10]

As Gitler left at the end of his first visit to Keio, Kiyooka gave him a copy of his translation of Fukuzawa's autobiography and said, "Maybe, Mr. Gitler, you would like to read this book about Fukuzawa Yukichi. He's the founder of this university, and it will give you a rather complete information about what the concepts are here at Keio University."

That night Gitler stayed up late reading the book. He was inspired, and he now had no doubt that Keio was the right choice. "I didn't really have a second choice," he later wrote. "Keio was the one place where it looked hopeful that it would go on. . . . I think I must have felt like Brigham Young felt when he reached the Great Salt Lake and said, 'This is the place!'"[11]

The next day Gitler wrote to Robert Downs, "As far as the location of the school in the city of Tokyo is concerned, at this writing it would seem to me that its establishment at Keio would make for a much healthier development of librarianship and our concept of librarianship in Japan." A week later, Paul Burnette, now back in the United States working under Downs at the University of Illinois library, wrote to Gitler, "Bob Downs and I feel as you do about Keio." Fortunately, Keio also emerged in first place in the numerical scores on the sixteen criteria Gitler had developed.

Gitler visited Keio again on January 17 and in a letter to Kiyooka dated January 22,[12] he enumerated his expectations:

1. Keio would perpetuate the school after June 30, 1952.
2. The school would have full status as a department in the faculty of literature.
3. Admissions would be handled jointly by the university admissions office and by the staff of the school.

4. Transfer students could be accepted from other colleges.
5. The school's course credits would be fully acceptable within the university.
6. The school course credits combined with three other years of study would be acceptable for a bachelor's degree.
7. Space would be remodeled as necessary.
8. Classroom equipment and furniture would be provided as needed.
9. ALA would support American staff from the army contract.
10. SCAP would support Japanese staff, except for janitorial and maintenance staff.
11. ALA would provide supplies and equipment.
12. Keio would provide scholarships to students in the school on the same basis as for other departments.

In another note on January 22, he expressed his confidence in Kiyooka: "If I may say so, professor Kiyooka, it is because I believe so very much in your ability at Keio to 'get things done' together with your very forward-looking spirit that I am in hopes that we shall be able to establish our Library School program at Keio." The same day, Gitler submitted to Nugent and Don Brown his report recommending Keio, and that choice was agreed the next day. Brown already thought that Keio was the best choice, but had chosen not to say so to Gitler.

On January 29 Keio's president, Ushioda Koji, confirmed Gitler's terms in writing; and on February 5 they were made formal by Nugent, on behalf of SCAP.

STRAIN AT KEIO

Gitler was insistent that the program be a regular university department on an equal standing with other academic departments within the university, even though it was a field that had not yet been accepted as an academic field in Japan. Keio also had to commit to assuming full responsibility for indefinite funding after the initial army contract expired. In addition, classroom and office space would be needed. Keio accepted all of these requirements. Gitler had additional expectations that were a strain for Keio, which was an elite, male university that admitted students from a relatively narrow social elite. Gitler insisted on admission of a diverse student body from across Japan, including female students and transfer students. (The admission of transfer students had been completely unacceptable at Tokyo University.) Being determined that the school should not be or appear to be an American school located in Japan, he also insisted that the new department be named The

Japan Library School, instead of Department of Library Science, which the university administration preferred.

Gitler, not knowing Japanese, and being unfamiliar with Japanese ways, found the negotiations frustrating. On February 6, he wrote to Downs, "From the standpoint of working with the indigenous group here, I must confess that on Saturday I thought it might be more advisable to abandon our project than to endeavor to carry it on subject to too many restrictive features. That problem we successfully solved by my taking a very strong personal stand—which proved to be the right move." He sent a carbon copy of this letter to John Cory at ALA headquarters with an added handwritten note: "At the moment I feel as if I were pushing against a great dead weight but once we dislodge the blocks I believe we shall make progress at a more respectable pace."

It was not only Keio. The Ministry of Education also had to be persuaded. It is reasonable to believe that it was Kiyooka who mediated and resolved issues at Keio and Don Brown at SCAP general headquarters who could bring pressure on the Ministry. Without the kind of help that Kiyooka and Brown provided, it is unlikely that Gitler could have succeeded. On February 10, 1951, SCAP issued a press release:

> *Librarians training school to begin soon at Keio University under the direction of the American Library Association.*
> Professional training of librarians comparable to that given in the United States has been made possible in Japan for the first time through establishment of a library school in Keio University which for the next 15 months will be under the direction of the American Library Association, according to a joint announcement made today by SCAPS's Civil Information and Education Section and the university.
> The school, believed to be the only one outside the United States teaching American library concepts and practices, will begin a one-year course in April on the Mita campus with a staff of six Americans headed by Robert L. Gitler, on leave from the University of Washington, where he is director of the School of Librarianship. . . . It is believed they will constitute the largest full-time foreign staff ever used in a regular professional school in any Japanese university.
> A least a reading knowledge of English will be helpful to students, according to Professor Gitler, but it will not be an absolute requirement for enrollment. . . . Lt. Col. D. R. Nugent, Chief of the Civil Information and Education section, said that SCAP had helped to establish the school because of recognition that Japan needed better librarians and that without them the high aims of the national Library law, which lays the foundation for library service in all communities, would be defeated.
> His selection of Keio as the university of which the library school would become a part, according to Professor Gitler, was influenced partly by his belief that the school and Japanese librarianship in general needed the liberal and forward-looking spirit inherited by Keio from its founder, Yukichi Fuku-

zawa. He was impressed also by the willingness to make whatever administrative adjustments the project might require, and by its agreement to continue the school after the period of American Assistance.

Gitler confided in a letter to Ludington on February 13,

> Even after everything had been signed and sealed there was a week of post-negotiations. . . . I selected Keio even though I was aware that they had practically nothing in the western sense in bibliographic and reference materials. Kyoto is far superior on this score. Yet all factors considered, it seemed to me that the prospects for success will hang so much on the will to continue, the educational climate, and the caliber of the personnel in charge of the university concerned. This is going to be even more true after the Occupation dissolves gradually into a thing of the past.
>
> A week ago Saturday I had to make a very determined stand to the extent of actually proposing the abandonment of the entire project. I found myself being so restricted by the traditional pattern and reluctance of the Japanese educators to comprehend what it is we are trying to do, that I earnestly believed we should not try to carry this through. This action, which was no stage-play on my part, proved to be the correct action, and I have had relatively clear sailing on the academic front since that time. You see, it is very important that we blend and integrate this program into the current Japanese university structure to the furthest degree possible in order to provide the best chance for its carrying on successfully when we are no longer here. Naturally one encounters many difficulties in this process . . . although the matter of transfer had been carefully explored over the past months, by everyone who has been interested in the project, the effecting of the details is something which I still believe the Ministry of Education views with great alarm and suspicion.

In March he reported a further crisis to her. The Ministry of Education required a detailed description of a four-year program before it would give its blessing to the new degree. Gitler refused and started to make arrangements to meet personally with the minister. This move induced ministry staff to approve the degree with less detail.[13]

ENGAGING WITH JAPANESE LIBRARIANS

In addition to ALA, SCAP, and Keio, Gitler was concerned to establish good relations with Japanese librarians, many of whom had no, or limited, formal professional qualifications. Despite the goodwill Keeney and the CIE information center librarians generated, they might well feel threatened by the high formal standards of Gitler's program or resentful of it as an alien imposition. The new Library Law had changed the rules on them. Almost immediately when the school started, representatives of the Tokyo Library Association asked for a meeting, which was held at the University of Tokyo. Gitler and his faculty met with some two hundred Japanese librarians. The interpreter, Kawaguchi Aiko, used diplomatic language, but Gitler could sense anxiety, even hostility, in the questions. Concerned, he discussed the situation with his colleagues afterward. Gitler had great confidence in the faculty that he had assembled and he believed that Japanese librarians would be reassured if they had more contact with them. He used a policy, a plan, and a speech.

The policy was what he called "constant availability": in addition to regular office hours, his and the faculty's home addresses were made known, and everyone was expected to be available to answer questions at any time.

The plan was to take his faculty the length and breadth of Japan during the summer break offering workshops for existing library staff at no charge.

The speech was in response to an invitation to speak at the forthcoming Japan Library Association annual meeting in Tokyo. Gitler believed professional associations were important. He participated in them eagerly and encouraged others to do the same. "I'd always been a great go-to-meeting person professionally as indoctrinated by Sydney Mitchell," he said.[14]

Gitler accepted the invitation to speak and, drawing on past experience in amateur dramatics, considered how he could have maximum impact. He quickly decided he should present it in Japanese, so he wrote a short statement in English explaining the philosophy and the intended role of the school and how he believed it could help the development of librarianship in Japan. He then asked the highly educated Fujikawa Masanobu, whom he considered an exceptionally effective translator, to create a version of his speech in elegant Japanese. Gitler memorized a Romanized transliteration and rehearsed its presentation over and over again, coached by Fujikawa, trying to get the cadence and emphases as they should be.

It caused some confusion when Gitler started by apologizing for not knowing Japanese. He explained that he felt that this speech ought to be in Japanese and so he had had it translated. He then gave his speech, spoken, not read, in fluent, eloquent Japanese. His speech was well-received and was followed by a reception at which much sake was consumed. From then on, he enjoyed a friendly cooperative relationship.

NOTES

1. This chapter and the next are based on that book, Robert L. Gitler, *Robert Gitler and the Japan Library School: An Autobiographical Narrative* (Lanham, MD: Scarecrow Press, 1999), esp. chaps. 8–11.

2. Gitler to Ludington, December 5, 1950. ALA Archives, box 23: International Relations Office and Japan Library School, hereafter "ALA."

3. Gitler, *Robert Gitler*, 93–94.

4. The selection process is described in Gitler, *Robert Gitler*, chap. 8.

5. Jeffrey K. Ruoff, "Forty Days across America: Kiyooka Eiichi's 1927 Travelogues," *Film History* 4 (1990): 237–56.

6. Described by his wife, Sugimoto Chiyono, *But the Ships Are Sailing—Sailing—* (Tokyo: Hokuseido Press, 1959); and Kenneth J. Ruoff, "The Making of a Moderate in Prewar Japan: Kiyooka Eiichi" (undergraduate thesis, Department of East Asian Studies, Harvard University, 1989).

7. Sugimoto Etsu, *A Daughter of the Samurai: How a Daughter of Feudal Japan, Living Hundreds of Years in One Generation, Became a Modern American* (New York: Doubleday, Page, 1925); Hirakawa Setsuko, "Etsu I. Sugimoto's 'A Daughter of the Samurai' in America," *Comparative Literature Studies* 30, no. 4 (1993): 397–407; Georgina Dodge, "Laughter of the Samurai: Humor in the Autobiography of Etsu Sugimoto," *MELUS* 21, no. 4 (Winter 1996): 57–69.

8. Kiyooka Chiyono, *But the Ships Are Sailing—Sailing—*.

9. Suzuki Yukihisa, "American Influence on the Development of Library Services in Japan 1860–1948" (PhD diss., University of Michigan, 1974), 69–73.

10. Fukuzawa Yukichi, *Wikipedia*, https://en.wikipedia.org/wiki/Fukuzawa_Yukichi.

11. Gitler, *Robert Gitler*, 69.

12. Gitler to Kiyooka, January 22, 1951. Copy at Keio University, Library and Information Science Department.

13. Gitler to Ludington, March 10, 1951, ALA.

14. Gitler, *Robert Gitler*, 111.

Chapter Fourteen

The Japan Library School

We are occupied constantly and evenings when I am not at Keio we are engaged in some public relations or social activity with Japanese librarians or university people. . . . We have found ourselves receiving wonderful response from all whom we come into contact. —Robert Gitler, 1951

OPENING

The Japan Library School's inauguration ceremony was held on Saturday April 7, 1951, in the Enzetsukan, the public speaking hall, on Keio's Mita campus.[1] The Japanese national anthem was played by the Wagner Society, a Keio student band. There were speeches in English or in Japanese by Keio President Ushioda Koji; Director Gitler; a representative of Dr. Amano, the minister of education; National Diet Librarian Kanamori; and Colonel Nugent. Then the Keio alma mater song was sung with the Wagner Society band. A reception followed. Kiyooka had wanted the program to include "The Star-Spangled Banner," but Nugent had objected.[2]

In his speech, Gitler invoked the spirit of Keio's founder, Fukuzawa Yukichi, which had so inspired him:

> Japan has had libraries. She still has libraries, but by and large until 1946 these libraries were in the continental (European) tradition. They emphasized the storage and preservation of their treasures, but not the use and distribution of their holdings. Japan, in carrying forward her march toward her new goals needs many more libraries desperately, and she needs librarians to apply open and progressive concepts of library service in the library agencies she already has . . .
>
> Our being here on this campus and in this Hall is indeed most appropriate. This is, I understand, the only one of the original Fukuzawa structures spared during World War II. And, interestingly enough, it is a replica of the Early

American Meeting Hall where ideas were expressed, issues debated, policies determined, in the early American community. Some seventy-five years ago Fukuzawa Yukichi built this structure for not dissimilar purposes. Fukuzawa was a great man of his era.

. . . It was Fukuzawa who maintained a fervent devotion to western learning, not for Western learning in itself, but because of what the record of Western learning held that could be of value for Japan. He pursued this course of action at a time when there was hostility to things foreign and in times when Samurai swords cut men down with but little provocation. It was Fukuzawa who said, "As I see it, our own Keio-gijuku stands for Western studies in Japan as much as Dejima did for Dutch nationalism. Whatever warfare may harass our territory, we have never relinquished the hold on Western learning. As long as this school of ours stands, Japan remains a civilized nation of the world. Let us put our best efforts into our work . . ."

Indeed it is good to be here.[3]

The front cover of the school's first *Announcement Catalogue* reflected Gitler's sense of symbolism (see figure 14.1). At the top was Keio's logo, two crossed pen nibs, an allusion to the Latin motto that Fukuzawa favored: Calamus Gladio Fortior, meaning the pen is mightier than the sword. Lower down, a drawing of books showing Keio University held in place by the U.S. government on one side and by the American Library Association on the other. This rather heavy-handed symbolism was not repeated the next year. Inside, the invocation of Fukuzawa is also explicit:

This new venture is in the true Keio spirit and tradition of its revered founder, Fukuzawa Yukichi, one of the first truly modern men of Japan. He was liberal and progressive in his thoughts and actions in a time when it took great courage to stand apart from the crowd as an individual with new and creative ideas. His aspirations for Keio were high and far-seeing. It is in this forward looking tradition of Fukuzawa that the American Library Association is founding the Japan Library School within the framework of the Faculty of Literature on the Mita campus of Keio-gijuku.

Another section titled "What is meant by Library Science, Librarianship, Library Studies" reflected Gitler's sense of its mission. It concluded:

The professional librarian—the graduate of a library school—is the purveyor of library science and through the channel of the institution of the library he becomes the practitioner of librarianship, just as a doctor is a practitioner of medicine.

In short, Library Science offers preparation for a career to the person who has a broad education and who is keenly interested in books, people and life. Success and great personal satisfaction will be the reward of the librarian who is an outgoing, friendly person, who is intelligent, tolerant, imaginative and quick in understanding, and who is interested in making his contribution to the forward progress of Japan through the medium of Library Service.

Figure 14.1. The Japan Library School announcement catalog, 1951.

Instruction began a few days later on April 16 with 59 students from a wide geographical spread. The 595 inquiries concerning admission resulted in 79 applications judged favorably, most of whom were admitted without further examination.

Chapter 14
FACULTY

Gitler's gregarious nature and his regular, active engagement in professional associations had resulted in a wide circle of contacts. As director of the University of Washington library school, he would have been a regular participant not only in American Library Association meetings but also the Association of American Library Schools, the principal gathering of the faculty of these schools. Before he left for Japan, he was able to draw on these contacts to select quickly and carefully the initial set of U.S. faculty. Although he wanted the best teachers, he also was very concerned about how they would behave in relation to the Japanese.

He had two quite different criteria. Naturally, he expected them to be excellent in their field and effective as teachers. But he also was very concerned about their motivation and attitude. Going to Japan for a year would be an attractive adventure, but he did not want that to be a primary motivation. As for attitude, Gitler, as a Californian, would have been well aware of past prejudices against Asians and the unconstitutional internment of more than one hundred thousand Japanese Americans, mostly U.S. citizens, in remote concentration camps called "relocation centers." Also, of course, Japan recently had been an enemy nation with a reputation for wartime atrocities. Negative attitudes had to be avoided. For this reason, he wanted only individuals whom he knew already personally. He later explained:

> Without exception, I knew every one of these people, and most of them knew each other from AALS, the American Association of Library Schools. I think they were all known to each other. I recall one of the very first things I tried to convey was the reason why they were chosen. First they had demonstrated, and were well known for, their professional expertise. Second, I felt because of what I had known of them as individuals, as human beings, they had no prejudices of any kind with respect to the Japanese milieu.[4]

American visiting faculty, Gitler wrote to Downs in 1952, could be men or women, but "they must be 'right' people."[5] He later wrote of one candidate, "she may be too much of a perfectionist to be able to flex and make the compromise that one must frequently be ready for here."[6] During his years as director of the school, the only appointee whom he felt to be less than fully satisfactory was the only one he had not known personally and had accepted on the basis of a recommendation.

His first invitation was a telephone call to a favorite recent graduate of the University of Washington program, Phyllis Jean Taylor (now Jean Boucher), who was working as a reference and circulation assistant in the Territorial Library of Hawaii in Honolulu. He asked her to be the library school's librarian.

Frances Neel Cheney (1906–1996) was then associate professor in the library school at the George Peabody College for Teachers in Nashville, Tennessee. She had degrees in sociology and library science and years of experience as head of the reference department in the Joint Universities Library in Nashville. Active in professional associations, she had published many reviews of reference works as editor of the "Current Reference Books" section of the *Wilson Library Bulletin*, and she later wrote a respected guide to reference works.[7]

Bertha Margaret Frick (1894–1975) was an associate professor teaching cataloging and classification at Columbia University's School of Library Service. A mathematics teacher turned librarian, she had years of experience in the Columbia University libraries where she specialized in cataloging special collections. She was also an expert on illuminated manuscripts.[8]

Hannah Hunt (1903–1973) was then young people's librarian at the Rockford Public Library in Illinois. She had many years of experience as a storyteller and in providing library service to children and young adults, both in public libraries and in school libraries, as well as library extension work in Hawaii.[9]

Edgar Raymond Larson (1914–?) had prior experience in Japan working in the allied military government. With a degree in French and after several years' experience teaching in elementary and secondary schools, he had

Figure 14.2. Robert Gitler and Phyllis Jean Taylor (later Jean Boucher), in the Japan Library School library.

changed careers. A recent graduate of Gitler's library school at the University of Washington, he was working as a bibliographer at the Library of Congress through its prestigious internship program. He had an interest in audiovisual media.[10]

Part-time Japanese visiting lecturers were used; for example, Doi Shigeyoshi taught the classification and cataloging of Japanese and Chinese materials.

At an early staff meeting before the school opened, Gitler stressed that the "attitude of American faculty to Japanese personnel and all persons with whom we come in contact should always be tactful, in keeping with our principles of democratic living, considerate of their background and customs, and ever alert to the fact that we are being judged by our every word and act."[11]

Gitler and his visiting U.S. faculty colleagues, then, were on a conscious and idealistic mission to help librarianship develop in Japan in a way that they believed would be in the best interests of Japan. They all would have seen librarianship as having a social and political force as part of the arsenal of democracy. The strongest motivation was to help make Japan a more modern and more democratic country. Therefore, they were engaged in what they believed to be a very worthy and important cause beyond the technical intricacies of library science. Further, not only would they be training future library leaders of Japan, but also future library science faculty. However, they faced some difficulties:

- they knew little or no Japanese, and they had much to learn about Japanese customs and practices;
- they could only ever be in an advisory, supportive role;
- they would have to draw on their very different experience in the United States;
- they were greatly dependent for effectiveness on their advisers, such as Don Brown, Professor Kiyooka, and the translators and interpreters assigned to them; and
- being funded by the U.S. Army, they were associated with the occupation.[12]

Gitler himself, with his sense of performance, symbolism, and outreach, understood the need for early courtesy calls to the minister of education and the National Diet librarian and the importance of seeking to achieve the support of the Japanese library establishment. He saw great symbolism in naming the school the Japan Library School, contrary to the wishes of the Keio University administration. He insisted that instruction be only in Japanese. He imposed his policy of absolute availability on his U.S. colleagues.

The Japan Library School 123

Figure 14.3. Japan Library School first-year faculty and students. Front row center: Hannah Hunt, Bertha Frick, Robert Gitler, Frances Cheney, Jean Taylor (later Boucher), and Edgar Larson.

He emphasized what he felt Japanese librarians most needed: a sense of service. This is why he was so emphatic on providing workshops on reference service. Gitler continued his goodwill efforts relentlessly, writing to Downs at the end of June:

> We are occupied constantly and evenings when I am not at Keio we are engaged in some public relations or social activity with Japanese librarians or university people. I believe we have really cracked the chrysalis in this past month. We have found ourselves receiving wonderful response from all whom we come into contact. In fact in some regards I am getting support in the dark and cluttered corridors of the Japanese ministry, where I find frequent blocks and stoppages in the more sanitary portals of the SCAP. At least I have two typewriters and two new electric fans as evidence of this statement.[13]

CURRICULUM AND RESOURCES

Gitler was determined that it be the *Japan* Library School, and it was emphasized that students were not required to know English. But his imported faculty could only teach in English. As a result, all of the American faculty's teaching had to be interpreted in the classroom, and curricular materials were compiled in or translated into Japanese or compiled as needed. So, for example, the standard text on cataloging in American library schools—Akers's *Simple Library Cataloging*—was translated, and a bilingual glossary of library terms was compiled.[14]

But, in addition, works of a more philosophical nature were translated. For example, Pierce Butler's *Introduction to Library Science* (1933), a manifesto insisting that library science should be made more scientific and focus on the social impact of libraries, was translated.[15] Viewed in retrospect Butler's short book now seems ahistorical and curiously empty of content because the field's achievements were not explained. It was an argument in favor of the aspirations of the research-oriented graduate library school at the University of Chicago and highly regarded in the three decades after its publication.

Two inspiring testaments to the important social role of librarians were also translated: José Ortega y Gasset's "The Mission of the Librarian" (1935) and Archibald MacLeish's "Of the Librarian's Profession," published in the *Atlantic Monthly* in 1940.[16] Later on, J. Periam Danton's booklet *Education for Librarianship* (1946) was added.[17]

The curriculum is shown in table 14.1. It reflected the typical offerings of an American library school at the time, with the addition of specialized courses on Japanese and Chinese books.[18] Downs described the intended orientation of the school:

> The consensus is that the new school should stress the usually-neglected public service and social aspects of library work, producing children's and young people's librarians, readers' advisors, good reference librarians (with some knowledge of science and technology), and extension and regional librarians. The concept of effective library service is largely unknown in Japanese libraries, and one of the most useful functions of the new school will be to demonstrate methods and to inculcate enthusiasm for this concept.[19]

The initial foundational course, titled "Libraries, librarians and society," emphasized the social mission of libraries; another, with a similar emphasis, "Social (adult) education and the library," followed. The full slate of courses is shown in the table.

During the summer recess, CIE information center librarians provided very valuable experience for the school's students by providing internships in situations of exemplary library service.

Well-furnished space was made available within the Keio University library, and a thousand books for the library school's library were promptly ordered, with more to follow. A good library school program also needs access to a good array of reference works for student exercises. The Keio University library was found to have many useful works, and in May 1951 the U.S. Department of the Army granted an additional $10,000 for the purchase of general reference works published by U.S. publishers as an additional resource for the library school. Paul Burnette, who was by now working for Robert Downs at the University of Illinois library, assisted in the acquisition of materials; after he left Illinois, Ben Bowman, then at the Newbury Library in Chicago, took over.

REFERENCE WORKSHOPS

The school was intended to train good librarians for modern libraries on a nationwide scale, but it also saw itself as a service center for library science for the whole country. This latter role was addressed by organizing seminars and workshops, to provide research materials for in-service librarians, and, when necessary, to give them advice.[20]

Gitler led his faculty members in organizing twelve workshops in conjunction with the Ministry of Education during the summer of 1951, which at least a hundred librarians attended. Two other institutes reached 120 library staff, and some 250 attended other shorter institutes. Gitler's enthusiasm for outreach was sustained. As a colleague later commented, "Whenever circumstances would permit it, he gladly accepted invitations from various Japanese libraries, willing to give advice and delivered lectures."[21] Kiyooka estimated that Gitler and his faculty reached another two thousand library staff through other lectures and presentations in the first year.

Table 14.1. Japan Library School List of Courses, 1951–1952

No.	Re.	Title	Professor	Units
100	R1	Libraries, Librarians and Society	Gitler	2
101	R2	Social (Adult) Education and the Library	Gitler, Larson	2
102	R2	The Organization Administration and Management of Libraries	Larson, Cheney	2
110	R1	Cataloging and Classification of Library Materials (Technical Processes of the Library)	Frick	3
111	R1	Classification and Cataloging of Japanese and Chinese Materials (Part I)		1
112	R2	Advanced Cataloging and Classification of Library Materials	Frick	3
113	R2	Classification and Cataloging of Japanese and Chinese Materials (Part II)		1
120	R1	Informational and Bibliographic Sources and Methods	Cheney	3
121	R1	Japanese and Chinese Materials (Part I)		1
122	R2	Informational and Bibliographic Sources and Methods, Including Reference Service	Cheney	3
123	R2	Japanese and Chinese Materials (Part II)		
130	E1	Book Selection and Reader's Advisory Service	Cheney, Larson	2
140	E1	The School Library and Its Management	Hunt	2
150	R1	Library Work with Children and Young People	Hunt	2
151	E2	Children's Literature and Story Telling	Hunt	2
160	E1	Audio-Visual Materials in Library Service	Larson	2
170	E2	Library Service for Farm (Rural) Areas and Villages—Regional Library Service	Hunt	2
180	E2	The History of Books and Libraries	Frick	2
190	E2	Education for Librarianship: The Library School and Its Students	Cheney, Gitler, Staff	2
200	E1	Practice and Observation	Gitler, Staff	

R = Required; E = Elective; 1 = First semester; 2 = Second semester

In November 1951, in a letter to Flora Belle Ludington, Gitler wrote about Japanese librarians:

We try to understand their particular problems and appreciate as nearly as we can their unique thought processes. And the more we do this, the better we can serve them in assisting them in their approaches to new ways, means and above all concepts. Possibly we have extended ourselves too much—for when you get outside the walls and really get into the Japanese scene (libraries) you begin to realize what an enormous job they have ahead of them. You find, too, that there has been too much easy dismissal of Japanese librarians by Americans as being a completely negative factor in Japanese educational society. Not so. In fact I marvel at their industry with reference to certain persons and places.

We would do well if we had some American librarians with as much acumen as Shichi, for example, the Hd Libn of Kobe; as spirited and ethical a man as Nishimura Seiichi, of Kyoto Prefectural, etc. Of course they are exceptions, but they ARE! With the conclusion of the Summer Workshops we moved out for some short institutes which went very well. And this past six weeks I have been in Nagano, Osaka, Kyoto, Kobe and surrounding areas meeting with and talking to librarians – and all that goes with such a program. And I find that I have been able to work closely with and have good response from Monbusho.[22]

Shichi Kakuro (1909–1995) was head librarian of the Kobe City Library. He became the leader both of reference service in Japanese public libraries in the 1950s after being inspired by a lecture on reference by Frances Cheney at the Japan Library School, and he published a book on reference service that were read by many Japanese librarians. Nishimura Seiichi (1906–1981) was director of the Kyoto Prefectural Library, a leading library reformer, and an advocate for reference service.

A CRISIS AND DR. FAHS

The agreement with Keio was that the American staff (Gitler, the American faculty, and the librarian), were paid with U.S. funding, that Keio would pay Japanese staff, and that Japanese staff would replace the American staff. Gitler was rightly concerned that the American faculty needed to remain for longer than the initial funding allowed if the school was to be well-established and endure.[23]

In the meanwhile, negotiations for a Japanese peace treaty progressed, and it became increasingly evident that the Reorientation Branch in Washington and SCAP in Tokyo soon would cease to exist and, therefore, would not be able to provide any more support for the school. The State Department was approached as a source of continuing funding. In January 1952, the chairman of the ALA advisory committee for the school received word that the State Department would continue the school, and had included it in its budget. But on April 22 it was learned that the State Department, with a reduced budget, would be unable to provide funding. Therefore, no funding was available to pay the American staff after June 30, 1952, which was in the middle of the school year.

On April 23, Gitler was told of the cessation of funding, and he wrote despairingly to Downs: "In short we are 'caput mortuum.' For future American support is withdrawn according to intelligence received this date, and we shall have to turn over our students after June—to whom we cannot yet say."[24]

Charles Burton Fahs, who had suggested the National Diet Library mission, had left the State Department in 1946 to work for the Rockefeller Foundation. By 1950 he was its director for humanities.[25] John D. Rockefeller III had become deeply engaged in U.S.–Japan relations, and the Rockefeller Foundation was providing very extensive financial support to Japanese universities, so it would be the most obvious nongovernmental source of support.[26] Unfortunately, the foundation had made a strategic policy decision to discontinue funding library projects. Nevertheless, in May 1952 the Japan Library Association wrote to the foundation a letter endorsing the school in the strongest terms.

Fahs had a personal interest in libraries. As a Rockefeller program officer, he made it his business to be very well informed about all developments relating to the humanities. He made frequent fact-finding visits to East Asia, as his travel diaries record in detail. He had been monitoring the Japan Library School. "I was not present at the birth of the Japan Library School but I have followed its growth and development closely and with admiration during fourteen of the fifteen years of its life," he later wrote.[27]

ROCKEFELLER RESCUE

In the end, Fahs was able to persuade the Rockefeller Foundation to make an exception to its policy, and the Japan Library School was saved by a series of grants. First was an emergency award of $5,500 to support the school through December 1952, then $142,800 in decreasing annual installments through June 1956 to support one fewer American faculty member each year as Japanese replacements paid by Keio were hired. Finally, in 1956, an additional grant of $60,000 was made to support visits by foreign faculty over a five-year period starting in April 1957.

Gitler believed that the Rockefeller grant would not be awarded unless he stayed on as director. Unfortunately, the University of Washington was not willing to extend his leave beyond a second year, so he resigned from his position at the University of Washington, thereby losing significant pension benefits. Fahs later insisted that although continuity of leadership was a major concern, the foundation had not required Gitler to remain as director.

Figure 14.4. Dr. Fahs at Keio University, 1953. Front row, left to right: Sugimoto Chiyono, Florence M. Renny, President Ushioda Kouji, Charles Fahs, and Robert Gitler. Back row: Unidentified, Kiyooka Eiichi, and Hashimoto Takashi. Courtesy of the Rockefeller Archive Center.

Fahs intervened supportively again in 1954 when he wrote to the executive director of the American Library Association, now David Clift: "Miss Naomi Fukuda spoke to me about some of the problems which Mr Gitler has encountered. Her impression, like mine, is that Gitler is doing a very good job. She felt, however, that there was perhaps more which the ALA could do in a non-monetary way to recognize his work with the Library School at Keio in such a way as to give him additional moral support vis-à-vis . . . the world of librarianship in Japan."[28]

This resulted in a strongly worded letter commending Gitler's work sent to Keio's President Ushioda over the signatures of both the president of ALA, Quincy Mumford, and Executive Secretary Clift.

Gitler soon sent a note to Clift: "It seems more complimentary than I deserve. Yet, I confess it served—and will continue to serve—as a wonderful boost to my morale. . . . And, the statement was wonderfully worded as concerns Keio's present contribution and future responsibilities."

The Rockefeller Foundation also provided scholarships for Japan Library School faculty to study in the United States for a year. The first went to Nakamura Hatsuo, who had compiled a glossary of Japanese library science terms in 1951.

In a pamphlet issued by Keio University describing itself, the library school received prominent mention:

> At the conclusion of the Peace Treaty, the support of the Army was withdrawn, but finding that the American faculty was absolutely necessary to carry on the instruction, aid of the Rockefeller Foundation was solicited and granted. Since then the instruction has been gradually transferred to the Japanese faculty while the number of graduates has increased to several hundred.[29]

The Japan Library School was only one element in a larger mosaic, along with the information centers and the popular Institute for Educational Leadership (IFEL) training programs. In a sense, the Japan Library School was an anomaly. Its program was significantly more advanced than the mandated level, and its output was small in contrast to other programs. But the Japan Library School was important as a training ground for future library leaders.

NOTES

1. This chapter also follows Robert L. Gitler, *Robert Gitler and the Japan Library School: An Autobiographical Narrative* (Lanham, MD: Scarecrow Press, 1999). See also Robert L. Gitler, "Nihon toshokangaku kotohajme" [The Beginning of Library Science in Japan] in Madoko Kon and Masaya Takayama, *Gendai Nihon no toshokan kōsō: sengo kaikaku to sono tenkai* (Tokyo: Bensei Shuppan, 2013), 169–95; and Kon Madoko, "Intabyu: Nihon toshokan gakko no omoide" [Interview: Reminiscence of the Japan Library School], 317–30, in Kon and Takayama, *Gendai Nihon*.

2. Gitler to Downs, May 6, 1951, ALA.

3. Fukuzawa quotation is from Kiyooka's translation: Fukuzawa Yukichi. 1948. *Autobiography* (Tokyo: Hokuseido Press, 1948), 225.

4. Gitler, *Robert Gitler*, 75–76.

5. Gitler to Downs, July 2, 1952, ALA.

6. Gitler to David Clift, July 24, 1952, ALA.

7. For Cheney, see Robin Dodge and John V. Richardson, "Cheney, Frances Neel (1906–1996)," 47–49, in *Dictionary of American Library Biography, Second Supplement*, edited by Donald G. Davis (Westport, CT: Libraries Unlimited, 2003).

8. For Frick, see Jane Stevens, "Frick, Bertha Margaret (1894–1975)," 191–92, in *Dictionary of American Library Biography*, edited by Bohdan S. Wynar (Littleton, CO: Libraries Unlimited, 1978).

9. For Hunt, see Margaret Kaltenbach and John A. Rowell, "Hunt, Hannah (1903–1973)" 256–57, in *Dictionary of American Library Biography*, edited by by Bohdan S. Wynar (Littleton, CO: Libraries Unlimited, 1978); also, *ALA Bulletin*, 46 (November 1952): 332.

10. For Larson, see *Who's Who in Library Service*, 3rd ed. (New York: Grolier Society, 1955), 280.

11. Staff meeting [minutes], March 7, 1951.

12. Visiting American staff reminiscences include P. Jean Boucher, "A Time Long Ago in Tokyo (1951–1952): A Librarian Remembers," *SLA [Special Libraries Association] PNW Interface* (Winter 2003); Frances N. Cheney, "Grasshopper under a Helmet," *Wilson Library*

Bulletin 28, no. 3 (November 1953): 275–79; Gitler, *Robert Gitler*; Everett Moore, "Some Californians in Tokyo," *California Librarian* 14, no. 3 (March 1953): 167–69; Everett Moore, "Teaching in the Japan Library School," *College & Research Libraries* 16, no. 3 (July 1955): 250–53; Everett Moore, "A Certain Condescension?," *Library Journal* 85, no. 8 (April 15, 1960): 1528–31; and Anne Marie Smith, "Japanese Impressions," *Canadian Library Association Bulletin*, 10 (December 1953): 133.

13. Gitler to Downs, June 30, 1951, ALA.
14. Susan Grey Akers, *Simple Library Cataloging*, 3rd ed. (Chicago: American Library Association, 1944).
15. Pierce Butler, *An Introduction to Library Science* (Chicago: University of Chicago Press, 1933).
16. José Ortega y Gasset, "The Mission of the Librarian," *Antioch Review*, 21, no. 2 (Summer 1961), 133–54, https://www.jstor.org/stable/4610323.
17. J. Periam Danton, *Education for Librarianship: Criticisms, Dilemmas, and Proposals* (New York: School of Library Service, Columbia University, 1946), http://catalog.hathitrust.org/Record/001344230.
18. Takahisa Sawamoto, "Training and Education Programs for Librarians in Japan," 65–72, in *Library Education in Developing Countries*, edited by George S. Bonn (Honolulu: East-West Center Press, 1966).
19. *Oriental Collections, U.S.A. and Abroad. Report of the Third Group Meeting Held at the University of Pennsylvania, March 28, 1951*, sponsored by the Joint Committee of the Far Eastern Association and the American Library Association (Ames: Office of the Chairman, Iowa State College Library, 1951).
20. Takashi Hashimoto, "Japan Library School: Yesterday, Today, Tomorrow," *Library Science* (1965), 6.
21. Hashimoto, "Japan Library School," 6.
22. Gitler to Ludington, November 17, 1951, ALA.
23. Gitler to Downs, November 16, 1951, ALA.
24. Gitler to Downs, April 23, 1952, ALA.
25. For Fahs, see Rockefeller Archive Center, Charles Burton Fahs papers (FA099), *Collection Description*, 3, https://dimes.rockarch.org/xtf//media/pdf/ead/FA099/FA099.pdf.
26. Matsuda Takeshi, *Soft Power and Its Perils: U.S. Cultural Policy in Early Postwar Japan and Permanent Dependency* (Washington, DC: Woodrow Wilson Center Press, 2007).
27. Charles B. Fahs, "Congratulations to the Japan Library School on the Occasion of its Fifteenth Anniversary," *Library Science* (MITA), 4 (1966): iii.
28. Fahs to David Clift, July 15, 1954, ALA.
29. Keio University, International Liaison Department, *Keio University. General Information*. (Tokyo: Keio University, 1958), 9.

Chapter Fifteen

Afterwards

The efforts of the American instructors at the Japan Library School have been highly appreciated. —Takeuchi Satoru, 1979[1]

The Allied Occupation of Japan finally ended in April 1952. What happened to the individuals and institutions discussed in the previous chapters?

CALIFORNIA

The California county library system developed under James Gillis remains largely intact. The California State Library has the additional role of disbursing substantial federal funding for library purposes in California. After James Gillis's untimely death in 1917, he was succeeded by his deputy, Milton Ferguson, a less empathetic figure. An extended survey of library services in South Africa by Ferguson and Scottish librarian Septimus Pitt had a significant impact on the development of libraries there.

Harriet Eddy chose not to stay at the State Library after Gillis's death. She moved on to a long career in Berkeley, applying her organizational skills for the agricultural extension program administered by the University of California and specializing in home demonstrations. She remained actively engaged in left-wing progressive political movements and, like Keeney, had her passport confiscated for a while.

During the Cold War she tried with little success to advise Soviet-controlled socialist countries on library planning. In 1942, when visiting New York and Washington, a Yugoslav official had asked her to make a plan for unified library service and home demonstration work for use in his country after the war ended. She also was asked for a library plan for Bulgaria and soon after the war ended was invited to Sofia. A trip was planned but cancelled because of her sister's illness. When the Bulgarian Legation learned of her sister's death, the invitation was renewed.

Eddy took elaborate measures to avoid the attention of the Federal Bureau of Investigation. For example, she traveled openly to Stockholm, then surreptitiously took the train to her real destination. Her letters back to her closest friends in California either did not explain her travel or else were headed by cautions. For example, a letter from Europe in 1948 reporting on her travels and addressed "Dear Nearly Everybody," gave the return address as c/o American Express Co., 11 rue Scribe, Paris, France, and was marked "VERY CONFIDENTIAL. No Publicity Please." In it she explained "I am now on my way to Belgrade and Sofia. The invitations are entirely in the realm of cultural relations; to observe their library service, and discuss ways in which a unified library system might be adapted. Whether anything will happen cannot yet be predicted. So I am *very* desirous *not* to have this trip discussed." In 1956 she wrote to Carla Zimmerman, the California state librarian, about the "spread of influence" of the California county library system in the Soviet Union, Spain, Mexico, Yugoslavia, and Czechoslovakia. Her ideas for Yugoslavia were revised during a visit there in 1959.

Harriet Eddy remained a legendary figure among California librarians. Keeney certainly would have known about her achievements in implementing the California county library system, and they must have known each other personally. They both lived in Berkeley and shared the same strongly held, left-wing Progressive political views. Eddy lived to old age and died at age ninety in 1967.[2]

The American Library Association expanded its promotion of librarianship abroad and, with Rockefeller Foundation support, created the position of director of international relations. Encouraged by the success of the Japan Library School, ALA participated, with Ford Foundation support, in a similar venture in 1954: the creation of a new Turkish library school at the University of Ankara. Here, too, finding local faculty with acceptable academic qualifications was a problem, and the project failed.[3]

INFORMATION CENTERS

CIE information centers were turned over to the Department of State and assigned to the new U.S. Information Agency (USIA, known outside the United States as the U.S. Information Service, USIS). The USIA was a successor to the Office of War Information, established "to understand, inform and influence foreign publics in promotion of the national interest, and to broaden the dialogue between Americans and U.S. institutions, and their counterparts abroad."

Nineteen of the information centers were retained and designated American cultural centers. Holdings of these centers included 387,168 books, 20,000 government documents, 6,900 films, 9,294 filmstrips, 2,520,000 magazines (12,660 titles), 110,000 pamphlets, 72,000 news photos, 41,000 records, and 9,100 Voice of America transcriptions. In the twelve months beginning in October 1951, they had 13 million visits and annual book circulation of 70,000. In addition, audiovisual libraries in each prefecture were equipped with projectors, films, and audiovisual aids. The other information centers were converted into binational undertakings completely financed by the Japanese, with the USIS supplying trained local staff members and long-term loans of materials and equipment. These centers were an essential focal point of Japanese-American cultural activities. USIA activities expanded worldwide during the Cold War and then were phased out.

The many directors of individual information centers resumed library careers in the United States. Paul Burnette served for many years as director of the Army Library.

PHILIP KEENEY

Keeney was formally discharged from the army at San Francisco's Fort Mason without explanation on June 9, 1947. Being deemed a subversive during the Cold War anti-Communist "Red Scare" made him effectively unemployable. He decided to resume work in Europe on his scholarly study of libraries as a social force. He also tried to resume his role as adviser on the development of unified national library services. He sent prospectuses to at least fifteen foreign countries. His prospectuses were very similar to those of Harriet Eddy. As might be expected, Keeney and Eddy appear to have remained in contact with each other. Eddy listed Keeney's home addresses in successive personal address books, and among her papers is an undated greeting card from Keeney's wife, Mary Jane.

Keeney was prevented from going to Europe because the passport office continued to delay returning his passport to him. A lawyer advised him that a passport was not legally required to leave the country and that an identity document would suffice. So, he accepted an invitation to advise in Czechoslovakia and boarded the *Batory*, a ship bound for the Baltic port of Danzig. However, the FBI intervened and told the captain of the *Batory* that his ship would not be allowed to leave the harbor so long as Keeney was on board. Keeney was forced to disembark. He and Mary Jane became nationally notorious when they were forced to appear before Congress's House Un-American Activities Committee. Keeney invoked the Fifth Amendment, refusing to answer any questions about the Communist Party, and he was interrogated aggressively about the *Batory* episode. He and his wife became known as "the librarian spies," and he was subjected to unjustified assertions that he had engaged in subversive activities in Montana.

Keeney's left-leaning, Progressive views, developed in the 1920s and 1930s, would have seemed Communistic during the post–World War II Red Scare. No evidence of espionage has been made public, and the designation as spies appears to be an oversimplification and out of keeping with his prior career. Keeney and his wife did definitely hold left-wing views and like so many other academics and intellectuals of their generation would have sympathized with the aspirations of the Russian revolution and the dream of a new, more egalitarian society. Evidence indicated that when living in Berkeley they had attended Communist meetings in nearby Marin county, and in Washington they were regarded as actual or potential assets by known Soviet agents. On the other hand, designating anyone a spy for a foreign country implies unpatriotic actions. No charges were filed, and no evidence of acts of espionage have been made public.

Mary Jane was seen to hand a packet to a man identified as a Soviet spy. She did so openly, in public, and had a harmless explanation for it: She had brought back a publication from Europe for him. If the Keeneys really had been engaged in espionage, one might expect them to have been much more secretive in their behavior. The joint biography of the Keeneys accepts that they were spies and is titled *The Librarian Spies*. They may have been sympathetic to the aspirations of the Soviet Union and may have wanted to help, as Harriet Eddy had done through her consulting work. No charges were brought, no evidence made public, but with the very public accusations and lack of an honorable discharge status from the army, Keeney was unemployable in the prevailing atmosphere, guilty or not. He died in 1962.

JAPAN

The National Diet Library developed strongly and added an impressive branch, the Kansai Kan, in 2002.

The Library Law achieved in 1950 endured until modified in 2008. It was a mixed blessing. The requirement for professional qualifications was a significant achievement, but the standard was set so low that it institutionalized a low status for librarians. A role that required so little training would not command much respect, and the local government practice of job rotation around different departments inhibited the development of professional identity for librarians. Nevertheless, the librarian certificate programs became very popular, became widely available, and several thousand students completed the programs every year. In 2015 librarian certificate programs were being offered by 158 four-year universities and 58 junior colleges. Close to ten thousand students have received the librarian certificate annually, even though very few vacancies require that certification.

A School Library Law of 1953 generated a parallel program of certification for school librarians and, even more minimally, for teacher-librarians. In a development seemingly unique to Japan, there was an explosion of very small, private libraries for neighborhood children. This volunteer movement, known as *komodo-bunko*, was encouraged by school librarians because it promoted library use and awareness.[4]

The Training Institute at the Ueno library, which had been revived in 1947, went through many changes. It became the National Junior College of Library Science, moved to the new academic city of Tsukuba in 1999, and grew into a large University of Library and Information Science before becoming part of the University of Tsukuba in 2004.

The funding by the Rockefeller Foundation enabled the Japan Library School to develop steadily. As planned, each year it saw one fewer American visiting professor and one more Japanese career professor. In 1956, Robert Gitler stepped down, and Hashimoto Takashi took over as director. The Rockefeller Foundation made an additional grant in 1957 to strengthen the program, and the school moved to new quarters in 1962. In 1967 a new master's degree began. The name Japan Library School was retired in 1968 and Keio University adopted the form of name it had originally wanted, as a department of Keio University. It became the school of library and information science within the faculty of letters. The school began a PhD program in 1975.[5] Its advanced program exceeded requirements. In his detailed history of education for librarianship in Japan, Takeuchi commented on its impact: "This has represented an important advance in the development of library education in Japan. . . . Because of this thee-level program, library science has been given a passport to the academic world."[6]

The Keio and Tsukuba programs are regarded as the two most prestigious of the many schools now teaching library science in Japan. In a way the Keio program was undermined by the low requirements of the Library Law of 1950.

Kiyooka Eiichi continued his service and scholarly work at Keio and died in 1997, surviving his wife, Chiyono, by many years.

The bicultural and bilingual Naomi Fukuda remained highly influential. She worked as a freelance translator, then created and directed the library of the International House of Japan in Tokyo. She edited the *Guide to Japanese Reference Books*, the first such compilation, and numerous other works. Fukuda helped place young Japanese librarians in U.S. libraries supporting East Asian studies programs and acted as a mentor. Her advice included, "Never say 'I am busy.' It means that you are not capable." Fukuda returned to the University of Michigan as curator of the Japanese collection in the Asia

Library and retired to Hawaii, where she died in 2007 at nearly one hundred. The Order of the Precious Crown, Wistaria, was conferred on her in 1984.[7]

OTHER AMERICANS

Verner Clapp left the Library of Congress in 1956 to bring his initiative, energy, and wide-ranging experience to a unique new role. He became the founding president of the Council on Library Resources, a new philanthropic foundation established by the Ford Foundation to aid in solving problems of libraries—research libraries in particular—through research, demonstration projects, and dissemination. During his term as president, 1956 to 1967, $13 million was dispensed. He died in 1972. Charles Harvey Brown, already retired when he went with Clapp on the Diet Library mission, had died in 1960.

Robert Gitler stayed on at Keio until 1956. When he returned to the United States, he remained in education for librarianship, first as executive secretary of the American Library Association's board of education in which capacity he also served as secretary of the committee on accreditation until 1960. In the summer 1961 he returned to Keio as a visiting professor and conducted a series of field seminars.[8] In 1962 he became director of the department of librarianship at the State University of New York, Geneseo, then transferred to the directorship of the Peabody Library School at the George Peabody College for Teachers in Nashville, Tennessee, making him probably the only person ever to have been director of four different schools of librarianship. In 1967, feeling a need to look after his mother, he returned to San Francisco for his final professional position as university librarian at the University of San Francisco. He retired in 1975 but remained active. Throughout the period after leaving the Japan Library School, he was active as a consultant on library education and library administration, including a prolonged advisory role at Sophia University in Tokyo.

Don Brown and Donald Nugent both stayed to the end of the occupation. When SCAP was disbanded, Nugent continued in the military as information officer in the Far East Command. Don Brown remained in Japan after the occupation and engaged in cultural activities. He compiled a bibliography of English translations of Japanese literary works and published a newsletter, *Japan Queries & Answers*. He also served for thirty years as editor of the *Transactions of the Asiatic Society of Japan*. After he died in 1980, his books and papers became the Don Brown Collection in the Yokohama Archives of History, which published a catalog of his collection and a fine, well-illustrated biography of him.[9]

Charles Burton Fahs left the Rockefeller Foundation in 1961. After serving as an adviser at the U.S. embassy in Tokyo, he became director of international studies at Miami University near Cincinnati, Ohio.

RECOGNITION

The efforts of American librarians have been recognized and honored. In 1956 Keio conferred on Robert Gitler a rare honorary doctor of philosophy degree, only the thirty-fourth such award since the university was founded. To compensate him for his loss of pension rights at the University of Washington, alumni of the school created a special retirement fund that the university administration also supported. A scholarship fund that he had initiated with his own money was picked up and perpetuated in his name. The emperor of Japan conferred the Order of Sacred Treasure on Verner W. Clapp (1968) and Robert B. Downs (1983), and in 1990, the Order of the Rising Sun on Robert Gitler.

Philip Keeney received a glowing testimonial from the Japan Library Association and remains an honored figure among Japanese librarians. But, back in the United States, his supposed status as a Communist subversive made him unemployable, and he died in obscurity in 1962. His efforts to improve library services in Japan remained almost entirely unknown in the English language literature. Where his name was mentioned, usually it is in relation to the highly publicized allegations that he and his wife were Soviet spies. To add insult to injury, in the Soviet Union the principal library science journal, *Bibliothekar,* denounced him by name as an ignorant tool of reactionary capitalism.[10]

NOTES

1. Takeuchi Satoru, "Education for Librarianship in Japan: A Comparative Study of the Pre-1945 and Post-1945 Periods," (PhD diss., University of Pittsburgh, 1979), 158.
2. Eddy Papers, California State Library, Sacramento, box 2517, folder 8.
3. Robert B. Downs, "ALA Sponsorship of Library Schools Abroad: How to Start a Library School," *ALA Bulletin* 52 (June 1958): 388–400.
4. Ann M. Hotta, "Children, Books, and Children's Bunko: A Study of an Art World in the Japanese Context," (PhD diss., University of California, Berkeley, 1995).
5. For a detailed history through 1971, see Takahisa Sawamoto, "Keio University School of Library and Information Science: Its Past, Present and Future," *Library and Information Science*, 9 (1971): 11–23; and Satoru, "Education for Librarianship in Japan," 158.
6. Takeuchi Satoru, "Education for Librarianship in Japan," 182.
7. Biographical and bibliographical details of Fukuda and several tributes to her are in "In Memoriam—Naomi Fukuda (1907–2007)," special issue, *Journal of East Asian Libraries* 145 (2008), https://scholarsarchive.byu.edu/jeal/vol2008/iss145/; also Koide Izumi, "Catalyst for the Professionalization of Librarianship in Postwar Japan: Naomi Fukuda and the United States Field Seminar of 1959," *Asian Cultural Studies* 39 (March 2013): 65–78; Koide Izumi, "Fukuda Naomi to amerika toshokan kenkyu chosadan" [Fukuda Naomi and the American Libraries

Research Team], 213–48, in Madoko Kon and Masaya Takayama, eds., *Gendai Nihon no toshokan kōsō: sengo kaikaku to sono tenkai* (Tokyo: Bensei Shuppan, 2013); Madoko Kon, [Eulogy of Fukuda], *International House of Japan Bulletin* 27, no. 2 (2007): 46–48.

8. *Report of the Field Seminars on Education for Librarianship, July 17–August 13, 1961* (Tokyo: Keio University, Japan Library School, 1961).

9. *GHQ Jōhō Kachō Don Buraun to sono jidai: Shōwa no Nihon to Amerika*. [Don Brown as the chief of Information division of GHQ and the era], Yokohama Kokusai Kankeishi Kenkyūkai, Yokohama Kaikō Shiryōkan hen (Tokyo: Nihon Keizai Hyoronsha, 2009); and Yokohama Kaikō Shiryōkan, *Don Buraun to Shōwa no Nihon: Korekushon de miru senji, senryō seisaku* [Don Brown and the Showa Era in Japan: The War and Occupation Policies Depending on the Collection], Yokohama Kokusai Kankeishi Kenkyūkai, Yokohama Kaikō Shiryōkan hen (Yokohama-shi: Yūrindō).

10. B. Kozlovskii, "О японских библиотеках и их американскик попечителях" [About Japanese Libraries and Their American Patrons], *Bibliothekar* 50, no. 11 (November 1948): 31–36.

Chapter Sixteen

Summary and Retrospective

> Thus the library is presented to us as a sanctuary of free inquiry and objective search for truth. . . . Every healthy democracy must find itself in a continual process of gradual reform. —Wilhelm Munthe, 1939

Making some books available for others to read is a simple idea, but explanation becomes difficult as soon as we start to consider the varied motivations of the users, the purposes of the provider, and the impact of reading on beliefs and emotions. Further complications arise when the number of books and the number of readers become large. Examination of four kinds of purpose—fact checking, current awareness, historical research, and recreational reading—lead to different styles of library service. The traditional four types of library—university, public, school, and special—are characterized by their very different emphases on these four styles of library provision.

Libraries, as distinct from private book collections, are, with rare exceptions, a shared service. They are funded by some for others to use. So, library service is a political rather than a commercial, pay-to-read undertaking. Library budgets, as a result, are determined by the political priorities of funders and not defined commercially. Readers spend time rather than money. In consequence, tension and compromise arise between expectations of readers and purposes of the funders. The distinction between funders and readers is not simple because the same individuals may be active in both roles. Also, decision making becomes diffused because libraries are labor intensive and have hierarchical organizational structures that often are geographically decentralized.

Finally, reading is an interpretive and creative activity. We seek to make sense of what we see, and this sense-making is an aesthetic experience affecting our emotions as well as our beliefs. As a result, the effects of library use and, therefore, of library provision, generally are hard to ascertain, let alone evaluate.

HISTORICAL NARRATIVES

We started with Robert Gitler's journey to Japan to start a library school, which evolved into a broader curiosity about how other actors and factors influenced his mission. Here again, we quickly encounter complexity in the circumstances of library development in Japan and the role of related developments elsewhere, notably the development of public library service in rural California and the use of libraries abroad as a tool of foreign policy.

The events, individuals, and influences mentioned in the previous pages all deserve deeper examination. Description is easier than analysis. Nevertheless, some comments can be made. One is how tightly connected the U.S. actors were. Most of them knew each other personally prior to their involvement with Japan.

The narratives show forces in operation at multiple levels, and examples of leadership. In our account, Martin Schrettinger, James Gillis, Harriet Eddy, and Robert Gitler stand out. Apparent failures of leadership are equally present but much less visible and sometimes may be understood better as effectively leading in a different direction, as in the role of the Ministry of Education in the Library Law of 1950.

What might be regarded as fortunate and unfortunate accidents are part of the story. California readers benefited from the deadly labor dispute that induced James Gillis to abandon railroad management. Unspent funds in a military budget account created the opportunity for Don Brown to propose what became the Japan Library School. Philip Keeney suddenly was removed from his role as library officer because officials regarded him as a security risk. If he had been allowed to continue his work, the provisions of the Library Law might have been stronger and the future of public libraries and education for librarianship significantly different. We can speculate that in all of these cases similar developments likely would have occurred anyway in the long run. County libraries eventually would have developed in California anyway without Gillis, just not as soon and, probably, not so well. Substantial college-level education for librarians presumably would have developed in Japan without Gitler, but later and in some other way.

The adventures of the individuals involved makes for interesting narrative, but what they could do depended on the infrastructure of their environment. Laws and legislation concerning public libraries emerge as highly influential. The need for enabling legislation delayed Gillis's efforts in California, the rigid centralized institutional regime in France delayed development, and the limited provisions of the Library Law of 1950, although a welcome improvement, resulted in a weak development of public libraries and of library education in Japan for decades.

In turn, the institutional and infrastructural environment in any country is itself the product of deeply influential social traditions and cultural attitudes, as is seen in Hassenforder's analysis of the radically different development of public libraries in France compared with Great Britain and the United States. Acceptance of individualism, self-improvement, adult education, and liberal democracy are associated with American-style public library development. Emphasis on formal education, learning from instruction rather than by discovery, and totalitarian politics lead to different library development.

LIBRARIES IN JAPAN IN RETROSPECT

Japan resembles California geographically but with a much larger population. In relation to libraries, Japan shared some features with France. Both had a strong central government and weak local government authority, an emphasis on formal schooling and examinations, and a tradition of libraries that emphasized conservation rather than service and outreach. The Japanese tradition of conserving Buddhist and other treasured writings was very long and strong, but public library services in Japan before the occupation generally were small collections with closed or semi-closed access. Reference service was lacking except for a few metropolitan libraries. Libraries were valued as assemblages of collectibles or as resources for developing reading skills, and, in universities, served as an academic resource. They existed and operated largely in isolation. The infrastructure for effective interlibrary cooperation was lacking.

Training for library work was not a requirement for employment and, to the limited extent that training was available, it focused primarily on basic internal procedures for acquisition, cataloging, and classification. The service provided hardly needed more. Librarianship was not recognized as a profession. Local government staffing practices favored generalists who could be rotated between different departments rather than professional specialists qualified for a single role. Emphasis on a lending collection catering to readers' recreational demands reduced the scope and need for professional expertise. An educational and social mission requiring bibliographical tools, nonfiction book selection, reader assistance, and reference service would have needed more professional and subject expertise. In these aspects Japanese libraries differed in emphasis from the United States.

This situation should not be regarded as a choice that librarians made. Evidence is that leading Japanese librarians were well aware of library practices in the United States, Great Britain, and elsewhere. Some had visited the United States. A few had attended library schools outside Japan. Descriptions in Japanese of foreign librarianship were available, and enough librarians could read English-language library literature. They knew how libraries in the United States were and, in general, would have preferred Japanese libraries to be more like them.

Similarly, the difference cannot be attributed to library users. The popularity of the CIE information centers, even though they did not provide materials in Japanese, is evidence of that. So is the widespread buying and selling of secondhand books and the practice of reading books in bookstores. When a library is a treasure of collectibles, the desire for preservation, the need for security, and pride of possession are reasons to discourage readers' use, but the need remains for scholarly expertise in subject matter and historical bibliography. A library seen as a resource for the development of reading needs minimal cataloging and has no need to be large, complex, or up to date.

An educational system that is didactic, authoritarian, and prepares students for examinations requires a defined curriculum, disciplined instruction, and a focus on textbooks and lecture notes. In such a situation, a library can be seen as a distraction and a challenge to the teacher's authority. Exploratory, pupil-driven learning becomes a liability.

Technical education needs manuals, and engineers need documentation of standards, but in library terms both are quite limited needs. Nineteenth-century scholars, before the explosion of publication late in the century and the consequent expansion of bibliographical indexing and abstracting services, were expected, worldwide, to know what literature they needed from their reading, footnotes, exchange of offprints, personal contacts, and other noninstitutional means. Japanese universities largely followed the German pattern of a central library with numerous small, isolated collections in departments, each guarded by an autocratic professor.

A well-informed electorate and well-developed, up-to-date information services in the form of a free press and well-developed library services are considered necessary for a liberal democracy, but these conditions constitute threats for an authoritarian regime or a strongly conformist society. Centralized concentration of governmental power, the lack of effective local government autonomy, and an absence of effective democracy reduce the perceived need for local libraries. During the first half of the twentieth century, Japanese governance was hardly democratic and became decreasingly liberal. The Diet in pre-surrender Japan did not draft legislation. It approved legislation prepared for it by the Cabinet. The Diet had little need for library service until, with the new constitution in 1947, it suddenly became the source of national authority.

Lack of money was not really the impediment. Japan had the resources to become a major military power and to establish a large colonial empire. Allocation of funds follows any regime's priorities, regardless of what librarians would recommend or readers would prefer. In Japan the regime became increasingly authoritarian during a period in which library services were developing elsewhere. The pattern of library provision that existed in 1945 was to be expected and probably seemed adequate to those in the central government concerned with priorities in the allocation of funds.

Gitler's mission was marked by a fortunate coincidence of several different factors, any one of which could easily have been less favorable. Initiative and leadership clearly made a difference. Don Brown's initiative and the selection of Gitler for the assignment were important. Gitler's relentless dedication, sustained enthusiasm, and obvious goodwill were hard to resist, and he understood the need for these qualities in the visiting faculty he so carefully selected. Others considered for this mission would not have brought the same attitude or charm. The tradition of hospitality to Western ideas at Keio University, derived from its founder, Fukuzawa, and extended by his liberal-minded grandson, Kiyooka, provided an exceptionally receptive home for the school. The persistence of Charles Fahs was crucial for the school's survival. Different personalities in these roles probably would have resulted in a less fortunate outcome.

In his heart, Gitler had a greater ambition. He, like Keeney, wanted to transform libraries and librarianship in Japan, especially public libraries. With this broader ambition, Gitler had little impact, and it was a source of frustration for him for the rest of his life. Nevertheless, the Japan Library School, as the Ueno Park Library Training Institute had in its early days, attracted good students. They were influenced by his ideas and became leaders in the profession. In this way, the school he founded has had significant long-term influence on the profession, and for that reason Gitler remains a revered figure.

The development of libraries in Japan, as in France, was based on the national government's social policies and priorities. The leading librarians in both countries were aware of best practices elsewhere, but they lacked the power to implement them. The use of wire mesh in public libraries to separate books from readers that offended John Nelson can be regarded as delay in following U.S. practice. The rapid creation of the new National Diet Library is telling. Superficially, it might look as if U.S. consultants designed a copy of the Library of Congress in Washington, DC, but the consultants, Verner Clapp, Charles Harvey Brown, and, later, Robert Downs, stated emphatically that this was not the case. Even allowing for their diplomatic courtesy, there seems to be no reason to doubt them.

The contrast between the impressive development of the National Diet Library and the relatively feeble development of public libraries under the Library Law of 1950 and the related development of professional education reflects both the difference in discretion between a research library and recreational reading and between the administrative imperative of the Diet leadership and the limited enthusiasm of the Ministry of Education.

Chapter 16
AMERICAN LIBRARIANSHIP

Library techniques and technology are not inherently national in character, so we may ask what "American librarianship" might mean. It could mean the sum of library services within the United States, and we could examine how that differed from library services in, say, Great Britain, India, or Russia. Library service has been progressively homogeneous and standardized internationally, but in the mid-twentieth century the variety was greater. Library practice in the United States favored dictionary catalogs with verbal subject headings interfiled with entries for titles and authors. In Europe practices were more varied. Europe favored separate author and subject catalogs, and subject catalogs often were arranged by classification numbers with an index. Anglophone and north European countries favored free public libraries funded by local governments. Fees for access or borrowing were common in Japan. Open access to the stacks was much commoner in the United States and the United Kingdom than in Germany or Japan. A particular emphasis in the United States and the Soviet Union was the provision of librarians who not only handled reference inquiries but also a fuller readers' advisory service to help guide readers to the most suitable books.

But different technical practices have different affordances and, therefore, different consequences. So social values are implicated in the choice of techniques. Raynard C. Swank, a successor to Sydney Mitchell as dean of Berkeley's school of librarianship, served as director of ALA's international relations office from 1959 to 1961. A sensitive and perceptive observer with firsthand experience of foreign libraries, he attempted in 1962 to identify "international values in American librarianship."[1] He identified six characteristics of American librarianship that he perceived as valuable for export:

- The conception of the library as an *organization* of books: That is to say, more than a mere collection.
- The evolution of a library profession: Library services needed professionally trained librarians with a sense of professional responsibility.
- An attitude of service: Libraries serve people.
- A library should function as an educational institution: The library had an educational mission.
- Librarians had a specific role to advance intellectual freedom.
- The conception of organized information as a public resource and responsibility, which implies public funding.

These characteristics are primarily statements geared to enabling Western liberal purposes. That would make Swank's vision more or less unacceptable for library development in a Fascist, militaristic, or totalitarian regime. Lenin was an admirer of American public libraries, but, of course, he saw them as valuable tools for a social program that was not Western liberal democracy.

Flora Belle Ludington had started the first OWI library in India, worked for several months in the CIE in Tokyo in 1948, and encouraged Robert Gitler in his mission. She, too, reflected on the American contribution to library development abroad. In a detailed historical account of international engagements by American librarians, she emphasized "the American concept of libraries for all" and "the premise that every man is capable of acquiring an education and that liberal access to library materials would contribute to his continued education." She also emphasized open shelf collections, the abolition of fees, and bringing books to people, advisory help and reference assistance, local funding, and professional education for librarians.[2]

LIBRARIES AND LIBERAL DEMOCRACY

Swank and Ludington both offered more than technical advice. They also had a firm ideological position. Their view of libraries, especially public libraries, and their commitment to liberal democracy was and remains so deeply accepted in the United States that it has been taken for granted and it would seem odd to question it.

The techniques and technology of librarianship are easily transferable between countries, and yet we see differences in library services attributable to cultural differences. So, one might ask whether a pure, generic form of librarianship can exist. Our conclusion is that it cannot because it is inherent in the nature of library service that it is driven by the social and political context of both providers and readers.

Reading induces learning and stimulates new ideas, so libraries are leaky. Ideas leak in and leak out. In this sense, books, when available in variety in libraries, have an inherently liberal, even democratic bias. A Norwegian librarian, Wilhelm Munthe, made a statement to this effect. After funding many surveys by expert American librarians to advise on the development of library services in other countries, the Carnegie Foundation decided to try a reverse approach and commissioned Munthe to critique library services in United States. In the resulting report, Munthe is rather pessimistic about public libraries, which he saw as heavily engaged in providing light fiction to women. But he concludes with a striking tribute to the role of libraries, especially public libraries, in providing an environment that was not neutral. It favored the cause of democracy:

> *A factor in human progress.* Thus the library is presented to us as a sanctuary of free inquiry and objective search for truth. . . . Every healthy democracy must find itself in a continual process of gradual reform, as the result of a peaceful readjustment of values in people's minds. . . . It is a great blessing

when this work can go on quietly and without creating bitterness and strife. . . . Its significance is raised to a higher plane where it joins forces and purposes with the scholarly library in a common task. The business of the latter is to help scholars in their work of constantly extending the bounds of knowledge, and the public library's business is to help the people at large take possession of these new-won territories.[3]

It is an inspiring vision. But why the association of public libraries with Western liberal democracy? Because libraries as Americans know them are liberal *by design*. They are intended to educate through individual discovery. A carefully selected array of books is presented on open shelves, with a catalog, bibliographies, and librarians available to enable the reader to find more. The central mythic notion is of a balanced collection, and the fact that services are funded politically in the context of a liberal democracy. Consider even the tendency for less popular books to be visible on the shelves when more popular items are out on loan.

The European Enlightenment, narrowly understood, refers to ideas developed by intellectuals in and around the eighteenth century. More broadly it refers to the enduring tradition of Renaissance humanism that values the individual, scientific reasoning, attention to evidence, tolerance, and, eventually, civic liberties and liberal democracy. The American public library, like the American Revolution, is rooted in this ideology. We can understand the American public library service better by comparing it with alternative services that provide documents free to the public and are not rooted in liberal democracy. We could compare library services in countries with totalitarian political regimes, such as North Korea. But we do not need to look far, given the presence of social media platforms, to find library-like services offering documents to the public without charging fees.

YouTube is a good example. It has a commercial purpose and an algorithmic design. Documents in the collection are accepted, not chosen, by the provider. One can search, but the selection presented to the user, as if on a shelf, is driven largely by complex secret algorithms using physical similarities between representations of documents and detailed records of prior use of documents. A remarkable and useful service is provided, but it is a commercial venture designed to generate revenue for the provider from advertising revenue. A consequence of this economic and technical design is that documents that attract attention are more profitable for authors, advertisers, and the platform. This situation favors intriguing personal attacks, startling fake news, dramatically polarized opinions, and, generally, intolerance. The economic and technical design amplifies these features and leaves managers with limited ability and little incentive to mitigate them.[4]

The mere fact of providing service online is not a determining factor. Wikipedia, for example, is in the same Enlightenment tradition as the public library. Wikipedia articles are carefully curated by human editors and policies requiring respect for different points of view, independent evidence, avoidance of partisan perspectives, and continual correction.

Public libraries and YouTube both provide information services. But the ideologies that guide the delivery of those services are distinct. Guided by different socioeconomic realities and ideologies, public libraries and platforms such as YouTube make different choices about the technologies they use to deliver their services.

Nakai Masakazu, vice director of the National Diet Library, like others influenced by the Frankfurt School, thought that the Enlightenment project was doomed. Specifically, he argued that new media technology so pervaded our consciousness that the Enlightenment ideal of the rational, tolerant individual, attentive to evidence, had been overwhelmed. Knowledge and belief increasingly were constructed collectively through mass media. Individual subjectivity increasingly was a shared group subjectivity. The present influence of social media would not have surprised him greatly.[5]

The association of public libraries with liberal democracy, therefore, has been historically contingent on the political environment of public funding and the particular technology of paper books on open shelves. Continuation of this close association is uncertain with either a change of political context or a major change in technology.

We started with Robert Gitler in 1950 in the sunset of the paper-based library. Starting in the 1960s, the technological focus of libraries became digital techniques that can provide the same paper-based library services better. This is the usual first phase of adopting new technology. The second phase, using new technology to do different things better, has barely started. This situation is more than a technical challenge. It calls for a deeper understanding of ideology and libraries.

NOTES

1. Raynard C. Swank, "International Values in American Librarianship," 115-29, in Cornell University, Libraries, *The Cornell Library Conference: Pages Read at the Dedication of the Central Libraries, October, 1962* (Ithaca, NY: Cornell University Library, 1964).
2. Flora B. Ludington, "The American Contribution to Foreign Library Establishment and Rehabilitation," *Library Quarterly*, 24 (April 1954): 192–204.
3. Wilhelm Munthe, *American Librarianship from a European Angle: An Attempt at an Evaluation of Policies and Activities* (Chicago: American Library Association, 1939), 53–55.
4. For a broader analysis of ideological shifts in document provision, see Ronald E. Day, *Indexing It All: The Subject in the Age of Documentation, Information, and Data* (Cambridge, MA: MIT Press, 2014).
5. Philip Kaffen, "Nakai Masakazu and the Cinematic Imperative," *Positions Asia Critique* 26, no. 3 (2018): 483–515, https://doi.org/10.1215/10679847-6868253.

Appendix

Keeney's Plan

This is a transcription of a carbon copy typescript in Keeney's papers in Berkeley's Bancroft Library. Differences are very minor in wording, punctuation, and presentation between it and the text reprinted in Takeo Urata and Ogawa Takeshi, eds., *Toshokanhō seiritsushi shiryō* (Tokyo: Nihon Toshokan Kyokai, 1968), 433–38.

TRANSMITTAL SLIP

Memorandum to Lt. Col. E. H. Farr. 8 April 1946

The accompanying study for a Unified Library Service for Japan is the result of several conversations with Mr. Carnovsky when he was in Tokyo with the Education Mission and informal talks with several Japanese librarians. Its basic principles are similar to the California County Library System which has been used, in part, by many other states in the United States and several foreign countries.

Due to the great book losses in Japan, it will be impossible to rehabilitate many of the libraries in the immediate future. However, a beginning can be made, if this study is followed, wholly or in some measure.

A free public library movement is considered an important factor in advancing the democratic idea, hence any project supporting free libraries, which Japan has never had, at least according to American standards, seems to be of vital importance now.

I take pleasure, therefore, in presenting this study to you for your contemplation and advice.

[Signed] Philip O. Keeney

PLAN

Unified Library Service for Japan [8 April 1946]

The post-war development of Japan's resources for livelihood call for adult education to bring to the people, in the localities where they live and work, information and guidance to enable them to apply all kinds of knowledge including scientific and technological to their various tasks. Those who have previously lacked opportunities for education must be given the chance to make good those earlier deficiencies. Those whose formal education has been adequate will need to have their knowledge continually brought up to date in the fields of technology and science related to their occupations. The unified library system can be organized as a channel for such knowledge, capable of reaching the smallest community.

Purpose

The purpose of such a service is to bring about exchange of books between localities through a centralized organization, so that all may share in the total collection of books throughout an organized area. Thus the aim is to create a library system which will be (1) unified; (2) economical, available to all localities on an equal basis, and complete; (3) organized as an integral part of the total educational system, co-ordinate with the classroom; (4) available to adults studying outside the classroom.

Unit for Service

In order to realize these aims. it is necessary to choose a unit for service that will be large enough to provide adequately and efficiently the usual service and to employ a trained librarian. The logical unit for administration in Japan is the prefecture, or a group of prefectures organized into a region, while the local communities within the prefecture or region are the logical units through which the service is given to the people.

ORGANIZATION AND ADMINISTRATION

Administrative headquarters for such a unified library service are established in the principal city of the prefecture with a trained librarian in charge. Requirements for training may be waived, if a suitable candidate is not available, but should become operative as soon as library schools have candidates to recommend. The headquarters library constitutes the clearing-house for a library service in every community in the prefecture or region. Branches are established wherever needed, in order to reach every resident. A public library in a city or town becomes a branch of the regional or prefectural library. In communities where no library existed, a branch is established with a reading room, when needed. Branches may be located in schoolhouses, clubs, community centers, stores, postoffices, wherever the people have ready access to the service. The place chosen should be one which can be open throughout the year and as many hours each day for effective aid to readers.

The prefectural or regional librarian visits the communities of the area covered, employs local custodians; supplies books and other material, based on community needs and purposes; and subscribes to such magazines as will be useful. When books and other reading materials are no longer circulating, they are returned, wholly or in part, to regional headquarters, and another supply is sent. The supply returned becomes available for other localities. If a book or other material is wanted, that is not in the local collection, the custodian obtains it from the regional headquarters.

The prefectural or regional organization is, in turn, unified with the NATIONAL LIBRARY where there will be a union catalog of all books in Japan. A prefectural or regional headquarters requesting a book not obtainable within the prefecture or region may locate and obtain it through the national library. All service is free to the borrower as the sending library pays all transportation costs.

Thus no matter where one lives, he has access to all the library service within Japan making the service EQUAL; all library material is used as far as possible making the service ECONOMICAL; every possibility of filling a request is resorted to, making the service COMPLETE; and every unit of service—the already established public library, the school library, the prefectural and national libraries—is woven into one system making it completely UNIFIED.

UNION CATALOG

The binding force in this plan is the union catalog which is absolutely essential in filling special requests and in avoiding unnecessary duplication. To build up these various union catalogs every library within the prefecture or region that purchases books or any other circulating material in addition to those furnished by the prefectural or regional library headquarters library files with its particular prefectural or regional library headquarters library a card under the author's* name for each book owned or purchased; and a subject card for every other library possession which circulates, viz., maps, globes, pictures, specimens, records, films. These cards, together with those for all possessions of the prefectural and regional library, constitute the union catalog for each particular administrative area that the prefectural or regional librarian consults when a special request is received.

A minimum of two copies of each card is made for prefectural or regional and national libraries. The prefectural or regional library makes the same number for all of its accessions. Thus the national library has a union catalog of all library possessions in Japan. In turn the national library will eventually exchange cards with other countries. The actual number of cards in the national library is reduced by having a master card for each book on which an attendant stamps the name of all libraries owning the book. It may also be decided to list in the national union catalog only the unusual maps, globes and the like, as each prefecture or region will own ordinary materials.

SUGGESTED PROCEDURE FOR PUTTING THE PLAN INTO EFFECT

The plan here outlined and proposed is not offered as an experiment, but has been carried out in different parts of the United States, and in varying degrees of completeness in Mexico and Canada, as well as several European countries. It is adaptable to any country at any time, but is especially suitable when destruction has wiped out libraries and other means of education. To ensure widespread understanding of its provisions and co-operation in establishing it, it would seem desirable that the Minister of Education should first hold a conference of all librarians; and, then later, a larger conference attended by teachers, representatives of agriculture and cooperatives, trade unions, professional organizations, women's clubs, and representatives of other associations selected by the Minister of Education. An appropriate agenda of such meetings might be as follows:

1. Distribution of copies of the plan to all present, and its presentation by reading aloud without discussion until finished;
2. Explanation of the reasons for the plan by the Minister of Education who, in addition to mentioning its successful operation in other countries and its suitability in the immediate post-war period, might point out that all forms of library service may recover more quickly if pooled so that libraries may perform their full part in raising the level of education and making recreation more accessible. It may be said that "library material not in circulation is dead." Its usefulness is proportionate to its circulation. The slogan of a unified library service is "All for one, one for all."
3. General discussion of the plan by attendants at the conference.
4. Adoption of plan or vote of confidence in it.

5. Appointment by the Minister of Education of committees to arrange for suitable legislation and other necessary tasks.
6. Separation of the conference into prefectural groups to discuss the carrying out of the plan in each prefecture.

Following such a conference several related undertakings would need immediate attention. For example: (1) A census of all trained librarians in order to ascertain their adaptability and willingness in organizing and operating the unified library plan; (2) Immediate provision should be made for the establishment of an adequate Library School; (3) Study will be necessary to determine what constitutes a prefectural or regional unit of service; (4) Japan has 46 prefectures. Many are large enough to be units of a unified library service. Those which are too small or too thinly populated would be grouped into regional units. Units would largely conform to geographical differences. The entire area of Japan would be included in some prefecture or region, so that the essence of the plan as a complete service would be realized. Determination of this unit of service should probably be made through a survey conducted by a trained librarian with the assistance of a competent committee; (5) The unified library service would naturally supersede separately organized public libraries, school libraries, and, as far as possible, special libraries. University and college libraries would remain under the jurisdiction of their institutions. Their books, however, should be listed in the national union catalog, and when feasible, in the prefectural or regional union catalogs, hence all books in Japan would be accessible to all the people needing them for study or recreation.

Bibliography

MANUSCRIPT SOURCES

American Library Association Archives, University Library, University of Illinois at Urbana-Champaign, IL. Esp. box 23: International Relations Office and Japan Library School.
Harriet G. Eddy Papers, California State Library, Sacramento, CA.
Philip O. Keeney Papers, Bancroft Library, University of California, Berkeley, CA.
Rockefeller Foundation Archives, Rockefeller Archive Center, Tarrytown, NY.

PUBLICATIONS

Akers, Susan G. *Simple Library Cataloging*, 3rd ed. Chicago: American Library Association, 1944.
American Assembly. *Cultural Affairs and Foreign Relations*. Englewood Cliffs, NJ: Prentice-Hall, 1963.
American Library Association. *Conclusions and Recommendations of the International Relations Board*. Memorandum, [26] March 1947.
Anderson, Ronald S. *Japan: Three Epochs of Modern Education*. Washington, DC: U.S. Department of Health, Education, and Welfare, Office of Education, 1959.
"Armed Services Editions." *Wikipedia*, https://en.wikipedia.org/wiki/Armed_Services_Editions.
Bess, Demaree. "Tokyo's Captive Yankee Newspaper." *Saturday Evening Post* 215, no. 32 (February 6, 1943): 22 and 66.
Borer, Arline. "Japanese Marvel at Osaka Library Exhibit." *Wilson Library Bulletin* 23, no. 4 (December 1948): 310–11.
Bostwick, Arthur E. *The American Public Library*, 3rd ed. New York: Appleton, 1928.
Boucher, P. Jean. "A Time Long Ago in Tokyo (1951–1952): A Librarian Remembers." *SLA [Special Libraries Association] PNW Interface* (Winter 2003).
Bowen, Roger. *Innocence Is Not Enough: The Life and Death of Herbert Norman*. Armonk, NY: M. E. Sharpe, 1986.
Brewitt, Theodora R. "James L. Gillis 1857–1917," 74–84, in *Pioneering Leaders in Librarianship*, edited by Emily M. Danton. Chicago: American Library Association, 1953.
Brewster, Beverly J. *American Overseas Library Technical Assistance, 1940–1970*. Metuchen, NJ: Scarecrow Press, 1976.

Brown, Charles H. *Scientific Serials*. Chicago: Association of College and Reference Libraries, 1956.
Brown, Don. *Beginning of the School* [unedited transcript of talk given 28 November 1976].
Brundin, Robert. "Sydney Bancroft Mitchell and the Establishment of the Graduate School of Librarianship." *Libraries & Culture* 29, no. 2 (1994): 166–85.
Buckland, Michael K. *Library Services in Theory and Context*, 2nd ed. Oxford: Pergamon, 1988; also http://sunsite.berkeley.edu/Literature/Library/Services/.
———. "Library Technology in the Next Twenty Years." *Library Hi Tech* 35, no. 1 (2017): 5–10; also http://escholarship.org/uc/item/9gs9p655.
———. "On Types of Search and the Allocation of Library Resources." *Journal of the American Society for Information Science* 30, no. 3 (May 1979): 143–47.
———. "The Relationship between Human Librarians and Library Systems: Catalogs and Collections," 91–105. In *Estudios de la información: teoría, metodología y práctica*, cood. Georgina Araceli Torres Vargas. Mexico City: UNAM, Instituto de Investigaciones Bibliotecológicas y de la Información, 2018, http://ru.iibi.unam.mx/jspui/handle/IIBI_UNAM/L158.
Butler, Pierce. *An Introduction to Library Science*. Chicago: University of Chicago Press, 1933.
California State Library. *News Notes of California Libraries* (1906–1979). Sacramento: California State Library, 1–74.
California State Library, and James L. Gillis. *Descriptive List of the Libraries of California*. Sacramento: W. W. Shannon, superintendent of state printing, 1904.
Casey, Marion. *Charles McCarthy: Librarianship and Reform*. Chicago: American Library Association, 1981.
Cheney, Frances N. "Grasshopper under a Helmet." *Wilson Library Bulletin* 28, no. 3 (November 1953): 275–79.
Clapp, Verner W. "Mission to Japan." *Information Bulletin (Library of Congress)* (February 24–March 1, 1948): 7–8, https://catalog.hathitrust.org/Record/000639207.
———. "R. B. Downs Reports on the National Diet Library of Japan." *Library of Congress Information Bulletin* (September 21, 1948): 17, https://catalog.hathitrust.org/Record/000639207.
Cohen, Theodore. *Remaking Japan: The American Occupation as New Deal*. New York: Free Press, 1987.
Collet, Joan. "American Libraries Abroad: United States Information Agency Activities." *Library Trends* 20, no. 3 (January 1972): 538–47.
Correia, Kathleen, and John Gonzales. "Biographies of State Librarians from 1850 to the Present." *California State Library Foundation Bulletin*, 68 (Spring/Summer 2000): 1–18.
Creel, George. *How We Advertised America*. New York: Harper, 1920, https://catalog.hathitrust.org/Record/000005455.
Cull, Nicholas. *The Cold War and the U.S. Information Agency: American Propaganda and Public Diplomacy, 1945–1989*. Cambridge, UK: Cambridge University Press, 2008.
Danton, Emily Miller. *Pioneering Leaders in Librarianship: First Series*. Chicago: American Library Association, 1953.
Danton, J. Periam. "Corrigendum and Addendum to a Footnote on Library Education History," 73–78, in *Essays and Studies in Librarianship Presented to Curt David Wormann on His Seventy-Fifth Birthday*, edited by M. Nadav and J. Rothschild. Jerusalem: Magnes Press, Hebrew University, 1975.
———. *Education for Librarianship: Criticisms, Dilemmas, and Proposals*. New York: School of Library Service, Columbia University, 1946, http://catalog.hathitrust.org/Record/001344230.
Day, Ronald E. *Indexing It All: The Subject in the Age of Documentation, Information, and Data*. Cambridge, MA: MIT Press, 2014.
Dictionary of American Library Biography, *Supplement*, edited by Donald G. Davis, 1990. *Second supplement*, edited by Donald G. Davis, 2003.
Ditzion, Sidney Herbert. *Arsenals of a Democratic Culture: A Social History of the American Public Library Movement in New England and the Middle States from 1850 to 1900*. Chicago: American Library Association, 1947.

Dodge, Georgina. "Laughter of the Samurai: Humor in the Autobiography of Etsu Sugimoto." *MELUS* 21, no. 4 (Winter 1996): 57–69.
Dodge, Robin, and John V. Richardson. "Cheney, Frances Neel (1906–1996)," 47–49, in *Dictionary of American Library Biography, Second Supplement*, edited by Donald G. Davis. Westport, CT: Libraries Unlimited, 2003.
Domier, Sharon. "From Reading Guidance to Thought Control: Wartime Japanese Libraries." *Library Trends* 55, no. 3 (Winter 2007): 551–69.
Donaldson, Scott. *Archibald MacLeish: An American Life.* Boston: Houghton Mifflin, 1992.
Dormont, Marcelline. "The French Connection: Remembering the American Librarians of Post-WWI France." *American Libraries* (February 16, 2017), https://americanlibrariesmagazine.org/2017/02/16/french-connection-librarians-wwi-france/.
Dower, John W. *Embracing Defeat: Japan in the Wake of World War II.* New York: Norton, 1999.
Downs, Robert B. "ALA Sponsorship of Library Schools Abroad: How to Start a Library School." *ALA Bulletin*, 52 (June 1958): 388–400.
———. *National Diet Library. Report on Technical Processes, Bibliographical Services and General Organization.* Tokyo: National Diet Library, 1948.
———. *Perspectives on the Past: An Autobiography.* Metuchen, NJ: Scarecrow Press, 1984.
Du Mont, Rosemary R. *Reform and Reaction: The Big City Public Library in American Life.* Westport, CT: Greenwood, 1977.
Eddy, Harriet G. [Comments on James Gillis]. *News Notes of California Libraries* 52, no. 4 (October 1957): 712–13.
———. *County Free Library Organizing in California, 1909–1918.* Sacramento: California Library Association, 1955.
Edmonds, Anne C. "Ludington, Flora Belle (1898–1967)," 322–24, in *Dictionary of American Library Biography*, edited by Bohdan S. Wynar. Littleton, CO: Libraries Unlimited, 1978.
Elder, Robert E. *The Information Machine: The United States Information Agency and American Foreign Policy.* Syracuse, NY: Syracuse University Press, 1968.
Espinosa, J. Manuel. *Inter-American Beginnings of U.S. Cultural Diplomacy: 1936–1948.* Washington, DC: Government Printing Office, 1976.
Fahs, Charles B. "Congratulations to the Japan Library School on the Occasion of Its Fifteenth Anniversary," *Library Science* (MITA) 4 (1966): iii–iv.
———. *Government in Japan; Recent Trends in Its Scope and Operation.* New York: International Secretariat, Institute of Pacific Relations, 1940.
Fainsod, Merle. "Military Government and the Occupation of Japan," 287–304, in Douglas C. Haring, *Japan's Prospect.* Cambridge, MA: Harvard University Press, 1946.
Fayet-Scribe, Sylvie. "Women Professionals in France during the 1930s." *Libraries and the Cultural Record* 44, no. 2 (2009): 201–19.
Ferguson, Milton J. *Memorandum: Libraries in the Union of South Africa, Rhodesia and Kenya Colony.* New York: Carnegie Corp., 1929, http://catalog.hathitrust.org/Record/001165635.
Fukuzawa, Yukichi. *Autobiography.* Tokyo: Hokuseido Press, 1948.
"Fukuzawa Yukichi." *Wikipedia*, https://en.wikipedia.org/wiki/Fukuzawa_Yukichi.
Gaddis, John W. *Public Information in Japan under American Occupation: A Study of Democratization Efforts through Agencies of Public Expression.* Geneva: Imprimeries Populaires, 1950.
Garrett, Jeffrey. "Redefining Order in the German Library, 1775–1825." *Eighteenth-Century Studies* 33, no. 1 (Fall 1999): 103–23, http://www.jstor.org/stable/30053317.
Garrison, Dee. *Apostles of Culture: The Public Librarian and American Society, 1876–1920.* New York: Free Press, 1979.
GHQ Jōhō Kachō Don Buraun to sono jidai: Shōwa no Nihon to Amerika. [Don Brown as the Chief of Information Division of GHQ and the Era], Yokohama Kokusai Kankeishi Kenkyūkai, Yokohama Kaikō Shiryōkan hen. Tokyo: Nihon Keizai Hyoronsha, 2009.
Gillis, James L. "Relation of State Libraries to Other Educational Institutions." National Association of State Libraries. *Proceedings and Addresses. Eleventh Convention.* (1908): 29–30.

———. "Shall the State Library be Head of All Library Activities in the State?" National Association of State Libraries. *Proceedings and Addresses. Fourteenth Convention.* (1911): 12–13.
Gitler, Robert L. "Japan." *Library Trends* 12, no. 2 (October 1963): 273–94.
———. "Nihon toshokangaku kotohajme" [The Beginning of Library Science in Japan], 169–95, in Madoko Kon and Masaya Takayama, *Gendai Nihon no toshokan kōsō: sengo kaikaku to sono tenkai.* Tokyo: Bensei Shuppan, 2013.
———. *Robert Gitler and the Japan Library School: An Autobiographical Narrative.* Lanham, MD: Scarecrow Press, 1999.
Gurin, Ruth M., and H. M. Baumgartner. "U.S. Information Libraries Prove Their Worth," *Library Journal* 71, no. 3 (February 1, 1946): 137–41.
Haber, Samuel. *Efficiency and Uplift: Scientific Management in the Progressive Era, 1890–1920.* Chicago: University of Chicago Press, 1964.
Hadley, Eleanor M. *Memoir of a Trustbuster: A Lifelong Adventure with Japan.* Honolulu: University of Hawaii Press, 2003.
["Hannah Hunt"] *ALA Bulletin*, 46 (November 1952): 332.
Hansen, Debra G. "Depoliticizing the California State Library: The Political and Professional Transformation of James Gillis, 1890–1917." *Information and Culture* 48, no. 1 (2013): 68–90.
Hara, Kakuten. *Gendai Ajia kenkyū seiritsu shiron: Mantetsu Chōsabu, Tōa Kenkyūjo, IPR no kenkyū.* Tokyo: Keiso Shobo, 1984, 426–74.
Haring, Douglas G., ed. *Japan's Prospect.* Cambridge MA: Harvard University Press, 1946.
Harris, Michael. "The Purpose of the American Public Library: A Revisionist Interpretation of History." *Library Journal*, 98 (September 15, 1973): 2509–14.
Harsaghy, Fred J. "The Administration of American Cultural Projects Abroad." PhD diss., New York University, 1985.
———. "Seventy Million Japanese Say 'Yes.'" *Wilson Library Bulletin* 27, no. 4 (December 1952): 309–13 and 320; also letter, *Wilson Library Bulletin* 27, no. 6 (February 1953): 419.
Hart, Justin. *Empire of Ideas: The Origins of Public Diplomacy and the Transformation of U.S. Foreign Policy.* Oxford: Oxford University Press, 2013.
Haruyama, Meitetsu. "Kanamori Tokujiro to sousouki no Kokuritsu Kokkai Toshokan: sengo Nihon niokeru aru 'toshokangaku' no tanjo" [Kanamori Tokujiro and the Early National Diet Library: The Birth of Some 'Librarianship' in Postwar Japan], 39–85. In Madoko Kon and Masaya Takayama, *Gendai Nihon no toshokan kōsō: sengo kaikaku to sono tenkai.* Tokyo: Bensei Shuppan, 2013.
Hasenfeld, Yeheskel. *Human Service Organizations.* Englewood Cliffs, NJ: Prentice-Hall, 1983.
Hashimoto, Takashi. "Japan Library School: Yesterday, Today, Tomorrow." *Library Science* (1965): 6–11.
Hassenforder, Jean. "Comparative Studies and the Development of Libraries." *UNESCO Bulletin for Libraries* 22, no. 1 (1968): 13–19.
———. *Développement comparé des bibliothèques publiques en France, en Grande-Bretagne et aux États-Unis dans la seconde moitié du XIXe siècle (1850–1914).* Paris: Cercle de la librairie, 1967, http://barthes.enssib.fr/travaux/Caraco-Hassenforder-dvpt-compare-bib-publiques.pdf.
Hausrath, Donald C. "United States International Communication Agency." *Encyclopedia of Library and Information Science*, vol. 32 (1981): 70–112.
Heindel, Richard H. "U.S. Libraries Overseas," *Survey Graphic*, 35 (May 1946): 162–65.
Held, Ray E. "Gillis, James Louis (1957–1917)," 197–200, in *Dictionary of American Library Biography*, edited by Bohdan S. Wynar. Littleton, CO: Libraries Unlimited, 1978.
———. *The Rise of the Public Library in California.* Chicago: American Library Association, 1973.
Henderson, John W. *The United States Information Agency.* New York: Praeger, 1969.
Henshall, May D. "California County Free Library." *Library Journal* 54, no. 14 (August 1929): 643–46.

Heygood, William C. "Leon Carnovsky: A Sketch." *Library Quarterly*, 38 (October 1968): 422–28.
Hirakawa, Setsuko. "Etsu I. Sugimoto's 'A Daughter of the Samurai' in America." *Comparative Literature Studies* 30, no. 4 (1993): 397–407.
Hirschman, Albert O. *Exit, Voice, and Loyalty: Responses to Decline in Firms, Organizations, and States*. Cambridge, MA: Harvard University Press, 1970.
Histoire des bibliothèques françaises, edited by André Vernet and others. 4 vols. Paris: Promodis-Editions du Cercle du librairie, 1988–1992.
Holborn, Hajo. *American Military Government: Its Organization and Policies*. Washington, DC: Infantry Journal Press, 1947.
Holley, Edward G. "Charles Harvey Brown," 10–48, in *Leaders in American Academic Librarianship, 1925–1975*, edited by Wayne A. Wiegand. Pittsburgh, PA: Beta Phi Mu; and Chicago: American Library Association, 1983.
———. "Mr. ACRL: Charles Harvey Brown (1875–1960)." *Journal of Academic Librarianship* 7, no. 5 (November 1981): 271–78.
Hotta, Ann M. "Children, Books, and Children's Bunko: A Study of an Art World in the Japanese Context." PhD diss., University of California, Berkeley, 1995.
"In Memoriam: Naomi Fukuda (1907–2007)," special issue, *Journal of East Asian Libraries*, 145 (2008), https://scholarsarchive.byu.edu/jeal/vol2008/iss145/.
James, Henry. "The Role of the Information Library in the United States International Information Program." *Library Quarterly* 23, no. 2 (April 1953): 75–114.
"James Gillis." Special issue. *News Notes of California Libraries* 52, no. 4 (October 1957): 633–714.
Japan. Ministry of Education. *Progress of Education Reform in Japan.* Tokyo: Ministry of Education, 1950.
"Japanese Library School." *ALA Bulletin*, 44 (December 1950): 458.
"Japan's 'Library of Congress.'" *Library of Congress Information Bulletin* (July 27–August 2, 1948): 11–13, https://catalog.hathitrust.org/Record/000639207.
Jevons, Stanley. "The Rationale of Free Public Libraries." *Contemporary Review* 16, no. 3 (March 1881): 385–402. Reprinted in David Gerard, ed. *Libraries in Society: A Reader*. London: Bingley, 1978, 16–20.
Jochum, Uwe. *Bibliotheken und Bibliothekare 1800–1900*. Würzburg: Konigshausen und Neumann, 1991.
Joeckel, Carleton B. *The Government of the American Public Library*. Chicago: University of Chicago Press, 1935.
Johnson, Alvin S. *The Public Library: A People's University*. New York: American Association for Adult Education, 1938.
Kaffen, Philip. "Nakai Masakazu and the Cinematic Imperative." *Positions Asia Critique* 26, no. 3 (2018): 483–515, https://doi.org/10.1215/10679847-6868253.
Kaltenbach, Margaret, and John A. Rowell. "Hunt, Hannah (1903–1973)," 256–57, in *Dictionary of American Library Biography*, edited by Bohdan S. Wynar. Littleton, CO: Libraries Unlimited, 1978.
Kantor, Ken. "Japanese Libraries, American Style." *Wilson Library Bulletin*, 29 (September 1949): 54–55.
Keeney, Philip O. "Against Autocratic Library Management." *Library Journal* 59, no. 11 (April 1, 1934): 312–13.
———. "Democratic Aids to Staff Responsibility." *Library Journal* 59, no. 12 (April 15, 1934): 361.
———. "Japanese Librarians Are War-Damaged." *Library Journal* 73 (May 1, 1948): 681–84.
———. "Meet the Japanese Librarians." *Library Journal* 73 (May 15, 1948): 768–72.
———. "The Public Library: A People's University?" *Wilson Library Bulletin* 13, no. 6 (February 1939): 369–77 and 387.
———. "Reorganization of the Japanese Library System." *Far Eastern Survey* 17 (January 28, 1948): 19–22; and (February 11, 1948): 32–35. Reprinted in Takeo Urata and Ogawa Takeshi, eds., *Toshokanhō seiritsushi shiryō.* Tokyo: Nihon Toshokan Kyōkai, 1968, 419–33.

———. "The Responsibility of Being Head Librarian." *Library Journal* 59, no. 6 (March 15, 1934): 271–72.
Keio University. International Liaison Department. *Keio University. General Information.* Tokyo: Keio University, 1958.
Kendrick, Douglas M. "Don Brown," *Transactions of the Asiatic Society of Japan.* Third series, 15 (1980): 1–2.
Kiyooka, Chiyono. *But the Ships are Sailing—Sailing—.* Tokyo: Hokuseido Press, 1959.
Koide, Izumi. "Catalyst for the Professionalization of Librarianship in Postwar Japan: Naomi Fukuda and the United States Field Seminar of 1959." *Asian Cultural Studies*, 39 (March 2013): 65–78.
———. "Fukuda Naomi to amerika toshokan kenkyu chosadan" [Fukuda Naomi and the American Libraries Research Team], 213–48, in Madoko Kon and Masaya Takayama, *Gendai Nihon no toshokan kōsō: sengo kaikaku to sono tenkai.* Tokyo: Bensei Shuppan, 2013.
Kon, Madoko. "CIE infuomeshon senta no katsudo" [The Activities of the CIE Information Center], 87–154. In Madoko Kon and Masaya Takayama, *Gendai Nihon no toshokan kōsō: sengo kaikaku to sono tenkai.* Tokyo: Bensei Shuppan, 2013.
———. [Eulogy of Fukuda.] *International House of Japan Bulletin* 27, no. 2 (2007): 46–48.
———. "Intabyu: Nihon toshokan gakko no omoide" [Interview: Reminiscence of the Japan Library School], 317–30. In Madoko Kon and Masaya Takayama, *Gendai Nihon no toshokan kōsō: sengo kaikaku to sono tenkai.* Tokyo: Bensei Shuppan, 2013.
Kon, Madoko, and Masaya Takayama, eds. *Gendai Nihon no toshokan kōsō: sengo kaikaku to sono tenkai.* [The Library Conception in Modern Japan: The Postwar Reformation and Its Development]. Tokyo: Bensei Shuppan, 2013.
Kozlovskii, B. "О японских библиотеках и их американскик попечителях" [About Japanese Libraries and Their American Patrons]. *Bibliothekar* 50, no. 11 (November 1948): 31–36.
Kraske, Gary E. *Missionaries of the Book: The American Library Profession and the Origins of United States Cultural Diplomacy.* Westport, CT: Greenwood, 1985.
Kraus, Joe W. "The Progressive Librarians Council." *Library Journal*, 97 (July 1972): 2351–54.
Krummel, D. W. "Downs, Robert Bingham (1903–1991)," 79–82, in *Dictionary of American Library Biography: Second Supplement*, edited by Donald G. Davis. Westport, CT: Libraries Unlimited, 2003.
Larson, Cedric. "Books across the Sea: Libraries of the OWI." *Wilson Library Bulletin* 25, no. 2 (February 1951): 433–36.
Learned, William S. *The American Public Library and the Diffusion of Knowledge.* New York: Harcourt, Brace, 1924.
Lee, Robert Ellis. *Continuing Education for Adults through the American Public Library, 1833–1964.* Chicago: American Library Association, 1966.
Lucken, Michael. *Nakai Masakazu: Naissance de la théorie critique au Japon.* Dijon: Les presses du reel, 2016.
Ludington, Flora B. "The American Contribution to Foreign Library Establishment and Rehabilitation." *Library Quarterly*, 24 (April 1954): 192–204.
MacLeish, Archibald. "The Strategy of Truth," 19–31, in *A Time to Act: Selected Addresses*, edited by Archibald MacLeish. Boston: Houghton Mifflin, 1943.
Maptalk. n.p.: United States. Army. Forces, Far East, Information and Education Section, 1–5 (1944–1946) and *Supplements* 1–5 (1945).
Martin, Lowell. *Enlightenment: A History of the Public Library in the United States in the Twentieth Century.* Lanham, MD: Scarecrow, 1998.
Masakazu, Nakai. *Wikipedia*, https://en.wikipedia.org/wiki/Masakazu_Nakai.
Matsuda, Takeshi. *Soft Power and Its Perils: U.S. Cultural Policy in Early Postwar Japan and Permanent Dependency.* Washington, DC: Woodrow Wilson Center Press, 2007.
Matsumoto, Kiichi, "Libraries and Library Work in Japan," *ALA Bulletin* 20, no. 10 (October 1926): 243–44.
McClurkin, John B. "People and Books in Japan." *Alabama Librarian* 4 (July 1953): 18–19.

McMurry, Ruth E., and Muna Lee. *The Cultural Approach: Another Way in International Relations*. Chapel Hill: University of North Carolina Press, 1947.
McNelly, Theodore. *Origins of Japan's Democratic Constitution*. Lanham, MD: University Press of America, 2000.
McReynolds, Rosalee. "Trouble in Big Sky's Ivory Tower: The Montana Tenure Dispute of 1937–1939." *Libraries and Culture* 32 (Spring 1997): 163–90.
McReynolds, Rosalee, and Louise S. Robbins. *The Librarian Spies: Philip and Mary Jane Keeney and Cold War Espionage*. Westport, CT: Praeger, 2009.
Miksa, Francis. "The Interpretation of American Public Library History," 73–92, in *Public Librarianship: A Reader*, edited by Jane Robbins Carter. Littleton, CO: Libraries Unlimited, 1982.
Minear, Richard H. "Cross-Cultural Perception and World War II: American Japanists of the 1940s and Their Images of Japan." *International Studies Quarterly* 24, no. 4 (December 1980): 555–80.
Mitchell, Sydney B. *Mitchell of California: Memoirs of Sydney B. Mitchell Librarian, Teacher, Gardener*. Berkeley: California Library Association, 1960.
———. "The Public Library in the Defense of Democracy." *Library Journal* 64, no. 6 (March 15, 1939): 209–12.
Miura, Taro. "Don Buraun to sai kyouiku medeia toshiteno toshokan" [Don Brown and a Library as a Recurrent Education Medium], 197–212. In Madoko Kon and Masaya Takayama, *Gendai Nihon no toshokan kōsō: sengo kaikaku to sono tenkai*. Tokyo: Bensei Shuppan, 2013.
———. "Senryouka Nihon niokeru toshokanhou seitei katei" [The Enactment Process of the Library Law during Occupation in Japan], 249–70. In Madoko Kon and Masaya Takayama, *Gendai Nihon no toshokan kōsō: sengo kaikaku to sono tenkai*. Tokyo: Bensei Shuppan, 2013.
Mohrhardt, Foster. "Clapp, Verner Warren (1901–1972)," 77–81, in *Dictionary of American Library Biography*, edited by Bohdan S. Wynar. Littleton, CO: Libraries Unlimited, 1978.
Moore, Everett. "A Certain Condescension." *Library Journal* 85, no. 8 (April 15, 1960): 1528–31.
———. "Some Californians in Tokyo." *California Librarian* 14, no. 3 (March 1953): 167–69.
———. "Teaching in the Japan Library School." *College & Research Libraries* 16, no. 3 (July 1955): 250–53.
Morel, Eugène. *Bibliothèques, essai sur le développement des bibliothèques publiques et de la librairie dans les deux mondes*. 2e ed. Paris: Mercure de France, 1908, http://catalog.hathitrust.org/Record/001164300.
Mulhauser, Roland A. "Information Libraries Flourish in Japan." *Library Journal*, 73 (February 1, 1948): 160–63.
Mumm, Beulah. "California State Library School." *News Notes of California Libraries* 52, no. 4 (October 1957): 679–82.
Munro, Dorothea B. "Japanese Buzz Session." *Wilson Library Bulletin* 26, no. 4 (December 1951): 326 and 330.
Munthe, Wilhelm. *American Librarianship from a European Angle: An Attempt at an Evaluation of Policies and Activities*. Chicago: American Library Association, 1939.
Nelson, John M. "The Adult-Education Program in Occupied Japan 1946–1950." PhD diss., Department of Education, University of Kansas, 1954. Japanese translation *Senryōki Nihon no shakai kyōiku kaikaku*. Tokyo: Ōzorasha, 1990.
Ninkovich, Frank A. *The Diplomacy of Ideas: U.S. Foreign Policy and Cultural Relations, 1938–1950*. New York: Cambridge University Press, 1981.
Nugent, Donald R., ed. *The Pacific Area and Its Problems: A Study Guide*. New York: American Council, Institute of Pacific Relations, 1936.
Ochi, Hiromi. "Democratic Bookshelf: American Libraries in Occupied Japan," 89–111, in Greg Barnhisel and Catherine Turner. *Pressing the Fight: Print, Propaganda, and the Cold War*. Amherst: University of Massachusetts Press, 2012.
O'Connor, Peter. *The English-Language Press Networks of East Asia, 1918–1945*. Folkestone, UK: Global Oriental, 2010.

Ohsa, Miyogo. "On the Libraries in Japan." *ALA Bulletin* 20, no. 10 (October 1926): 244–51.
Oriental Collections, U.S.A. and Abroad. Report of the Third Group Meeting Held at the University of Pennsylvania, March 28, 1951. Sponsored by the Joint Committee of the Far Eastern Association and the American Library Association. Ames: Office of the Chairman, Iowa State College Library, 1951.
Orne, Jerrold, ed. *Research Librarianship: Essays in Honor of Robert B. Downs.* New York: Bowker, 1971.
Ortega y Gasset, José. "The Mission of the Librarian." *Antioch Review* 21, no. 2 (Summer 1961): 133–54, https://www.jstor.org/stable/4610323.
"Paul J. Burnette." *Library Quarterly* 27, no. 1 (January 1957): 48.
Pellisson, Maurice. *Les bibliothèques populairs à l'étranger et en France.* Paris: Imprimerie Nationale, 1906, https://catalog.hathitrust.org/Record/000961498.
Pincus, Leslie. "Revolution in the Archives of Memory: The Founding of the National Diet Library in Occupied Japan," 382–92, in *Archives, Documentation, and Institutions of Social Memory: Essays from the Sawyer Seminar,* edited by Francis X. Blouin Jr. and William G. Rosenberg. Ann Arbor: University of Michigan Press, 2006.
Price, Paxton, ed. *International Book and Library Activities: The History of a U.S. Foreign Policy.* Metuchen, NJ: Scarecrow Press, 1982.
Raber, Douglas. *Librarianship and Legitimacy: The Ideology of the Public Library.* Westport, CT: Greenwood, 1997.
Report of the Field Seminars on Education for Librarianship, July 17–August 13, 1961. Tokyo: Keio University, Japan Library School, 1961.
Richards, Pamela Spence. "Information for the Allies: Office of War Information Libraries in Australia, New Zealand, and South Africa. *Library Quarterly* 52, no. 4 (October 1982): 325–47.
Richardson, John V. "Harriet G. Eddy (1876–1966): California's First County Library Organizer and Her Influence on USSR Libraries." *California State Library Foundation Bulletin,* 94 (2009): 2–13, http://www.cslfdn.org/pdf/Issue94.pdf.
Roedel, Matilda A. "'Arigato,' say Japanese." *Library Journal,* 74 (December 1, 1949): 1792–95 and 1806.
Ruoff, Jeffrey K. "Forty Days across America: Kiyooka Eiichi's 1927 Travelogues." *Film History* 4 (1990): 237–56.
Ruoff, Kenneth J. "The Making of a Moderate in Prewar Japan: Kiyooka Eiichi." Undergraduate thesis, Department of East Asian Studies, Harvard University, 1989.
Sano, Tomosaburo. "The Public Library in Japan." *Public Libraries* 14, no. 6 (June 1909): 214.
Sawamoto, Takahisa. "Keio University School of Library and Information Science: Its Past, Present and Future." *Library and Information Science,* 9 (1971): 11–23.
———. "Training and Education Programs for Librarians in Japan," 65–72, in *Library Education in Developing Countries,* edited by George S. Bonn. Honolulu: East-West Center Press, 1966.
Schlipf, Frederick A. "Leon Carnovsky: A Bibliography." *Library Quarterly* 38, no. 4 (October 1968): 429–41.
Schneider, Douglas. "America's Answer to Communist Propaganda Abroad." *Department of State Bulletin,* 19 (December 19, 1948): 772–76.
Schrettinger, Martin. *Versuch eines vollständigen Lehrbuches der Bibliothek-Wissenschaft* (Munich: Author, 1808), 11, http://archive.org/details/bub_gb_x2qePg9yKNkCSchrettinger.
Schwantes, Robert S. *Japanese and Americans: A Century of Cultural Relations.* New York: Harper, 1955.
Shera, Jesse H. *Foundations of the Public Library: The Origins of the Public Library Movement in New England, 1629–1855.* Chicago: University of Chicago Press, 1944.
Smith, Anne Marie. "Japanese Impressions." *Canadian Library Association Bulletin,* 10 (December 1953): 133.
Stanionis, Arthur. "Illini and the War." *Daily Illini* (March 15, 1944): 2, col. 6, http://idnc.library.illinois.edu/cgi-bin/illinois?a=d&d=DIL19440315.2.27#.
Stephens, Oren. *Facts to a Candid World: America's Overseas Information Program.* Stanford, CA: Stanford University Press, 1955.

Stevens, Jane. "Frick, Bertha Margaret (1894–1975)," 191–92, in *Dictionary of American Library Biography*, edited by Bohdan S. Wynar, Littleton, CO: Libraries Unlimited, 1978.
Stielow, Frederick J. "Librarian Warriors and Rapprochement: Carl Milam, Archibald MacLeish and World War II." *Libraries and Culture* 25, no. 4 (Fall 1990): 513–33.
———. "MacLeish, Archibald (1892–1982)," 59–63, in *Dictionary of American Library Biography: Supplement*, edited by Wayne A. Wiegand. Englewood, CO: Libraries Unlimited, 1990.
Suggett, Laura S. *The Beginning and the End of the Best Library Service in the World*. San Francisco: San Francisco Publishing Co., 1924.
Sugimoto, Etsu. *A Daughter of the Samurai: How a Daughter of Feudal Japan, Living Hundreds of Years in One Generation, Became a Modern American*. New York: Doubleday, Page, 1925.
Sulllivan, Peggy. "Cory, John Mackenzie (1914–1988)," 55–58, in *Dictionary of American Library Biography: Second Supplement*, edited by Donald G. Davis. Westport, CT: Libraries Unlimited, 2003.
Supreme Commander for the Allied Powers. *History of the Non-Military Activities of the Occupation of Japan*. 55 vols. Tokyo, 1950–1952.
———. Civil Information and Education Section. Education Division. *Education in the New Japan*. Tokyo: General Headquarters, Supreme Commander for the Allied Powers, Civil Information and Education Section, Education Division, 1948.
———. Civil Information and Education Section. Education Division. *Post-war Developments in Japanese Education*. Tokyo, General Headquarters, Supreme Commander for the Allied Powers, Civil Information and Education Section, Education Division, 1952.
Suzuki, Yukihisa. "American Influence on the Development of Library Services in Japan 1860–1948." PhD diss., University of Michigan, 1974.
Swank, Raynard C. "International Values in American Librarianship," 115–29, in Cornell University Libraries. *The Cornell Library Conference: Pages Read at the Dedication of the Central Libraries, October, 1962*. Ithaca, NY: Cornell University Library, 1964.
Takayama, Masaya. *Rekishi ni miru Nihon no toshokan: chiteki seika no juyō to denshō* [Japanese Libraries in Modern History: Application and Inheritance of Intellectual Essence]. Tokyo: Keiso Shobo, 2016.
Takebayashi, Kumahiko. "Modern Japan and Library Movement." *Contemporary Japan*, 14 (April–December 1945): 224–43.
Takemae, Eiji. *Inside GHQ: The Allied Occupation of Japan and Its Legacy*. New York: Continuum, 2002.
Takeuchi, Satoru, "Education for Librarianship in Japan: A Comparative Study of the Pre-1945 and Post-1945 Periods." PhD diss., University of Pittsburgh, 1979.
———. "Japan, Education for Library and Information Science," 239–71, in *Encyclopedia of Library and Information Science*, vol. 36. New York: Marcel Dekker, 1983.
Tauber, Maurice F., and Eugene H. Wilson. *Report of a Survey of the Library of Montana State University for Montana State University, January–May 1951*. Chicago: American Library Association, http://hdl.handle.net/2027/mdp.39015034609811.
Thompson, Lawrence S. "Brown, Charles Harvey (1875–1960)," 63–65, in *Dictionary of American Library Biography*, edited by Bohdan S. Wynar. Littleton, CO: Libraries Unlimited, 1978.
Thomson, Charles A., and Walter H. C. Laves. *Cultural Relations and U.S. Foreign Policy*. Bloomington: Indiana University Press, 1963.
Thomson, Charles A. H. *Overseas Information Service of the United States Government*. Washington, DC: Brookings Institution, 1948.
Toshokan jōhōgaku kyōiku no sengoshi: shiryō ga kataru senmonshoku yōsei seido no tenkai [The Postwar History of Library and Information Science Education: The Development of Professional Training System Based on Materials]. Edited by Nemoto Akira. Kyōto-shi: Mineruva Shobo, 2015.
Truman, Harry S. "Termination of O.W.I. and Disposition of Certain Functions of O.I.A.A. Aug 31, 1945." *Department of State Bulletin* 13, no. 323 (September 2, 1945); 306–7.

Tung, Louise W. "Library Development in Japan." *Library Quarterly* 26, no. 2 (April 1956): 79–104; and no. 3 (July 1956): 196–223.

United States. Committee on Public Information. *Complete Report of the Chairman of the Committee on Public Information: 1917, 1918, 1919.* Washington, DC: Government Printing Office, 1920, https://catalog.hathitrust.org/Record/009600453.

———. Education Mission to Japan. *Report of the United States Education Mission to Japan. Submitted to the Supreme Commander for the Allied Powers, Tokyo, March 30, 1946*, 45. Washington, DC: Government Printing Office, 1946, https://catalog.hathitrust.org/Record/011325745.

———. Library Mission, and Supreme Commander for the Allied Powers. Civil Information and Education Section. 1948. *Report of the United States Library Mission to Advise on the Establishment of the National Diet Library of Japan.* Washington, DC: Government Printing Office, 1948, http://catalog.hathitrust.org/Record/009161030.

"United States Information Libraries Abroad." *Department of State Bulletin* 9, no. 223 (October 2, 1943): 228–29, http://catalog.hathitrust.org/Record/000598610.

Urata, Takeo, and Ogawa Takeshi, eds. *Toshokanhō seiritsushi shiryō*. Tokyo: Nihon Toshokan Kyōkai, 1968.

"U.S. Initial Surrender Policy for Japan." *Department of State Bulletin* 13, no. 326 (September 23, 1945): 423–27, https://catalog.hathitrust.org/Record/000598610.

Verner Warren Clapp, 1901–1972: A Memorial Tribute. Washington, DC: Library of Congress, 1973.

Vincent, J. C., J. H. Hilldring, and R. L. Dennison. "Our Occupation Policy for Japan." *Department of State Bulletin* 13, no. 328 (October 7, 1945): 538–45, https://catalog.hathitrust.org/Record/000598610.

Wachtel, Marion S. "Harriet G. Eddy." *California Librarian*, 28 (January 1967): 54–55.

Ward, Robert E., and Frank J. Shulman, eds. *The Allied Occupation of Japan, 1945–1952: An Annotated Bibliography of Western-Language Materials.* Chicago: American Library Association, 1974.

Welch, Theodore F. *Libraries and Librarianship in Japan.* Westport, CT: Greenwood, 1997.

———. *Toshokan: Libraries in Japanese Society.* London: Bingley, 1976.

Who's Who in Library Service. New York: H. W. Wilson, 4 eds., 1933–1966.

Wiegand, Wayne A. *Part of our Lives: A People's History of the American Public Library.* New York: Oxford University Press, 2015.

Willey, Malcolm M. "The College Training Programs of the Armed Services." *Annals of the American Academy of Political and Social Science*, 231 (January 1944): 14–28.

Williams, Edwin E. *International Library Relations: A General Survey of Possible Postwar Library Development.* Chicago: American Library Association, 1943.

Williams, Justin. "From Charlottesville to Tokyo: Military Government Training and Democratic Reforms in Occupied Japan." *Pacific Historical Review*, 51 (1982): 407–22.

———. *Japan's Political Revolution under MacArthur.* Athens: University of Georgia Press, 1979.

Williams, Patrick. *The American Public Library and the Problem of Purpose.* New York: Greenwood, 1988.

Williams, Robert V. "The Public Library as the Dependent Variable: Historically Oriented Theories and Hypotheses of Public Library Development." *Journal of Library History* 16, no. 2 (Spring 1981): 329–41; also, www.jstor.org/stable/25541199.

Winger, Howard. "Carnovsky, Leon (1903–1975)," 73–74, in *Dictionary of American Library Biography*, edited by Bohdan S. Wynar. Littleton, CO: Libraries Unlimited, 1978.

Winkler, Allan M. *The Politics of Propaganda: The Office of War Information, 1942–1945.* New Haven, CT: Yale University Press, 1978.

Witt, S. W. "Merchants of Light: The Paris Library School, Internationalism, and the Globalization of a Profession." *Library Quarterly* 83, no. 2 (2013): 1–21.

Yokohama Kaikō Shiryōkan. *Don Buraun to Shōwa no Nihon: Korekushon de miru senji, senryō seisaku* [Don Brown and the Showa Era in Japan: The War and Occupation Policies Depending on the Collection]. Yokohama Kokusai Kankeishi Kenkyūkai, Yokohama Kaikō Shiryōkan hen. Yokohama-shi: Yūrindō, 2005.

Index

Absher, Linda U., xi
adult education in Japan, 64, 69
Akers, Susan Grey, 98
All-Japan Library Conference, 1938, 89
allied occupation of Japan, 44–46, 46–47, 52. *See also* Civil Information and Education Section; Supreme Commander for the Allied Powers
American Library Association, 63; and libraries abroad, 134. *See also* International Relations Board
anti-communism, 73

Berkeley, CA, 23, 67–68. *See also* University of California, Berkeley
Boucher, Jean. *See* Taylor, Phyllis Jean
Brown, Charles Harvey, 79, 80–81, 81–83, 138
Brown, Don, 53–55; after allied occupation, 138; dismissed, 74; portrait, 54, 84; proposes library school, 97–98; and Robert Gitler, 106
Burnette, Paul Jean, 55, 100, 135; at Civil Information and Education Section, 81, 92; and Japan Library School, 100, 101, 111; and National Diet Library, 85
Butler, Pierce, 124

Cain, Julien, 19
California, 23; county library system, 1, 23, 29–31, 68–69; libraries in, 23. *See also* California State Library; University of California, Berkeley
California State Library, 23, 24–32, 69, 77, 133
Carnegie, Andrew, 15–16
Carnovsky, Leon, 62–63, 68
Cheney, Frances N., 121, 127
Civil Information and Education Section, 52–53. *See also* Education Mission; information centers; Japan Library School; Supreme Commander for the Allied Powers, , 63–64
Clapp, Verner W., 74, 80, 138, 139; and Japan Library School, 98–99, 100; and National Diet Library, 77, 79–80, 81–83
classification in libraries, 43
Clift, David, 129
Committee on Public Information, 35–36
Conference of Librarians of Imperial Universities, 1946, 74
Cory, John M., 98
county library system (California), 1, 23, 29–31, 68–69
Creel, George, 35–36
cultural contexts of library services, 13
culture and libraries, 13–20
Curti, Merle, 16

Danton, J. Periam, 124
Davis, Elmer, 38

democracy, 144; in Japan, 44–45, 144; and libraries, 15–16, 32, 89, 141, 148–149
Diet (Japan), 78–79. *See also* National Diet Library
Ditzion, Sidney, 14, 16
Doi Shigeyoshi, 122
Downs, Robert B., 86, 139; and Japan Library School, 100, 101, 111; and National Diet Library, 85

Ebert, Friedrich Albert, 10
Ecole des chartes (Paris), 19
Eddy, Harriet, 24, 27–29, 30, 133–134
education, 15, 144; in France, 19; in Japan, 41, 64, 69, 144; of librarians, 19, 23, 99; of librarians in Japan, 44, 90, 95, 98, 136–137, 143. *See also* Education Mission
Education Mission, 61–62, 64–65
equality, 15. *See also* democracy

Fahs, Charles B., 78, 128–129, 139, 145
Fairweather, Jane, 92
Ferguson, Milton, 31, 32, 133
Fisher, Vardis, 63
Fleischer, Benjamin, 53–55
Fleischer, Wilfred, 53–55
foreign policy, 35
France, libraries in, 17–20
Frick, Bertha M., 121
Fujikawa Masanobu, 115
Fukuda, Naomi, 44, 85, 86, 106, 137
Fukuzawa Yukichi, 108, 111, 117–118

Gaddis, John W., 53
Gillis, James, 24–27
Gitler, Robert L., 1, 105, 120, 138, 139, 145; compares Japanese universities, 106–108; and Japan Library School, 101–102, 117–118, 137; and Japanese librarians, 114–115, 118, 126–127; and Keio University, 111–113, 114; portraits, 107, 121, 129
Gompers, Samuel, 14
Graham, Mae, 72, 100

Hagen, R. P., 100
Hashimoto Takashi, 129, 137
Hassenforder, Jean, 17

Heindel, Richard, 38, 39
Hunt, Hannah, 121

information centers (Japan), 53, 55, 56–58, 134–135; in Osaka, 56; in Oyama, 57–58; in Tokyo, 56, 57; in Yokohama, 58
infrastructure, 77–78, 79, 81
Institutes for Educational Leadership, 98
International Relations Board (ALA), 99. *See also* Ludington, Flora Belle

Japan: adult education in, 64, 69; allied occupation, 44–46, 46–47, 52; librarians in, 47–48, 143; libraries in, 19, 41–44, 89, 91, 99; library users in, 144; propaganda in, 35. *See also* Ministry of Education (Japan)
Japan Library Association, 73, 115
Japan Library School, 1, 117–118, 123, 124–125, 127–128, 137, 145; *Announcement Catalogue*, 1951, 118–119, 119; curriculum, 124–125, 126; faculty, 120–124, 133; selection of Keio University, 106–112. *See also* Cheney, Frances N.; Doi Shigeyoshi; Frick, Bertha M.; Gitler, Robert L.; Hunt, Hannah; Larson, Edgar L.; Taylor, Phyllis Jean
Jevons, Stanley, 14
Joeckel, Carleton, 30, 32, 67–68
Johnson, Alvin, 31

Kanamori Tokujiro, 83–84, 86, 106
Kawaguchi Aiko, 115
Keeney, Mary Jane, 73, 135–136
Keeney, Philip O., 37, 63–64, 67–75, 135–136, 139; in California, 67–68; and Harriet Eddy, 134, 135. *See also* Unified Library Service for Japan
Keeney Plan. *See* Unified Library Service for Japan
Keio University, 108–109; University Library, 125. *See also* Japan Library School
Kiyooka Chiyono. *See* Sugimoto Chiyonon
Kiyooka Eiichi, 108–109, 110, 129, 137, 145
Krupskaya, Nadezhda, 17

Larson, Edgar R., 121
Learned, William S., 31
Lenin, Vladimir, 17
librarians, 9–10, 118; in Japan, 47–48, 143. *See also* education of librarians; libraries; library services
librarianship, 9, 146. *See also* libraries; library services
libraries, 3–8, 8–9, 16, 141; in California, 23; county library system (California), 1, 23, 29–31, 68–69; cultural contexts of, 13; and democracy, 15–16, 32, 89, 141, 148–149; and education, 89, 144; in France, 17–20; funding of, 16, 141, 144; in Japan, 19, 41–44, 89, 91, 99; Library of Congress, 37, 63, 74, 77, 80, 81, 82; in Mexico, 36; National Diet Library, 79–86, 136; provided abroad, 36, 36–37, 38–39; in the U.S., 14–16, 17–18, 19. *See also* information centers; library services; library users; national libraries; public libraries; school libraries; special libraries; university libraries
Library Law, 1899 (Japan), 41, 42
Library Law, 1950 (Japan), 90–95, 136
library mission, 81–83. *See also* National Diet Library
Library of Congress, 37, 63, 74, 77, 80, 81, 82; and National Diet Library, 81, 82
library officer, Civil Information and Education Section, 91. *See also* Burnette, Paul; Fairweather, Jane; Keeney, Philip O.
library science, 9, 146. *See also* libraries; library services
library services, 4–9, 10, 13. *See also* libraries
library users in Japan, 144
Ludington, Flora Belle, 38, 100, 106, 147

MacLeish, Archibald, 37, 74, 124
Mamiya Fujio, 78
Matsumoto Kiichi, 47–48
Mexico, reading rooms in, 36
Milam, Carl, 36, 38, 99
military government, 45–47
Ministry of Education (Japan), 71; and Japan Library School, 113, 114; and libraries, 89, 90; and Library Law, 1950, 142
Mitchell, Sydney, 31–32, 32–33, 34n8, 55, 68, 73; and Robert Gitler, 105
Mombusho. *See* Ministry of Education (Japan)
Morel, Eugène, 19–20, 49n8
Munthe, Wilhelm, 141, 147

Nakai Masakazu, 83–84, 84, 86, 149
Nakata Kunizo, 90
National Diet Library, 79–86, 136; and Library of Congress, 81
national libraries in Japan, 69, 70, 71, 78, 90. *See also* libraries; Library of Congress; National Diet Library
Nelson, John M., 91, 95
Nishimura Seiichi, 127
Nugent, Donald R., 70, 97–98, 106, 113, 138

occupation of Japan, 44–46, 46–47, 52. *See also* Civil Information and Education Section; Supreme Commander for the Allied Powers
Office of Facts and Figures, 37–38
Office of Strategic Services, 37
Office of the Coordinator of Inter-American Affairs, 36
Office of War Information, 37–39, 51
orientation of U.S. military, 45
Orne, Jerrold, 101
Ortega y Gasset, José, 124
Osaka, information center in, 56
Oyama, information center in, 57–58

Pellisson, Maurice, 20, 21n21
philanthropy and libraries, 16
Progressive Librarians Council, 63
public libraries, 61; and democracy, 148–149; in Japan, 42–43, 64–65, 91, 92; legislation, 142; in the U.S., 14–16, 20n12. *See also* libraries; Library Law, 1899; Library Law, 1950

reading rooms in Mexico, 36
reference services in Japanese libraries, 143
reference workshops in Japan, 125

Report of the United States Library Mission to Advise on the Establishment of the National Diet Library , 83
republicanism, 16. *See also* democracy
resource allocation in libraries, 8–9
Rockefeller, Nelson, 35
Rockefeller Foundation: grant to Tokyo University library, 99; and Japan Library School, 130, 137
Roosevelt, Franklin D., 35, 36

Shichi Kakuro, 127
scholar librarian, 9–10
school libraries, 43, 137. *See also* libraries
School Library Law, 1953 (Japan), 137
School of Librarianship, University of California, Berkeley, 31–32
Schrettinger, Martin, 9–10, 11n4–11n5
Shores, Louis, 101
special libraries, 43. *See also* libraries
Sugimoto Etsuko, 109
Sugimoto Chiyono, 109, 110, 129
Sullivan, John F., 51
Supreme Commander for the Allied Powers, 63–64. *See also* Civil Information and Education Section
Swank, Raynard C., 146, 147

Takebayeshi Kumanahiko, 42, 48
Takeuchi Satoru, 48, 95, 133

Taylor, Phyllis Jean, 120, 121
Tokyo, information center in, 56, 57
Tokyo Library Association, 114
Training Institute (Ueno), 137. *See also* Tsukuba, University of, , 137
Truman, Harry S., 51
Tsukuba, University of, 137

U.S. Education Mission, 61–62, 64–65
U.S. Information Agency, 134
U.S. Information Service, 134
Ueno Library Training School, 137
Unified Library Service for Japan, 68–71, 151–155
university libraries in Japan, 42, 65. *See also* libraries
University of California, Berkeley, School of Librarianship, 31–32
University of Tsukuba, 137
Ushioda Kouji, 129

Van Wagoner, Lou, 97–98, 106

Wada Mankichi, 44
Williams, Edwin E., 99
Willoughby, Charles, 73–74

Yokohama, information center in, 58
Yukawa Hideki, 58

www.ingramcontent.com/pod-product-compliance
Lightning Source LLC
Chambersburg PA
CBHW022013300426
44117CB00005B/173